Working Towards a Research Degree

Veronica Bishop
PhD, MPhil, RGN, FRSA

books

First published 1999 by Nursing Times Books
Emap Healthcare Ltd, part of Emap Business Communications
Greater London House
Hampstead Road
London NW1 7EJ

Printed and bound in Great Britain by Thanet Press Ltd, Margate, Kent

British Library cataloguing in Publication Data
A catalogue record for this book is available from the British Library.

ISBN: 1 902499 13 1

Contents

Foreword

Serving a research apprenticeship is a daunting, dizzying, as well as developmental experience. At times it seems more akin to the tale of the sorcerer's apprentice; overwhelming and out of control. Yet the paradox of learning to research is that, as with nursing according to Florence Nightingale, its elements are all but unknown. Mechanics are mentionable, recipes recordable in textbooks on the 'how to do' research. But too little is written of the micropolitics and processes of the 'degrees of development' involved in pursuing a research degree. This goes not only for nursing but other disciplines too. Studying for a research degree throws up many psychological and sociological challenges for our families, our friends as well as ourselves; stresses and strains we could never imagine or anticipate. Metaphors of travel, travail and transformation come to mind. What starts out as a voyage of discovery can also become, in the words of Graham Greene, a journey without maps. And nurses, for historical and political reasons, often have an especially tough assignment in undertaking research degrees. First is the anti-intellectual prejudice within and outside nursing. Second, a research degree has until recently been an exotic rather than 'natural' part of a nursing career, even in education. Third, many nurses come to research degrees later in life, often juggling family commitments and pursuing degrees on a part-time basis in conjunction with a full-time job. Fourth, many may not be versed or qualified in the discipline within which the research degree is pursued. The effect of any one of these would in itself be a strong enough disincentive to deflect the faint-hearted from pursuing a research degree. In nursing all or many of these attributes may be present in the profile of students. All the more credit should therefore be accorded to those who hold fast to this extraordinary course of development and find the courage to struggle with it. This book is an important 'travel companion' and hopefully comfort along the way. It will help to navigate the career path of a research degree through the experience of others. In doing so it is an important contribution to the 'lived experience' of research.

Dr Anne Marie Rafferty, April 1999

MEET THE CONTRIBUTORS

Foreword

Dr Anne Marie Rafferty studied for a BSc at the University of Edinburgh before working as a staff nurse in the Royal Infirmary, Edinburgh. She then moved to Queen's Medical Centre, Nottingham where she worked as a staff nurse and studied for an MPhil in clinical research for which she was awarded a *Nursing Times* 3M Health Care national nursing award in the research category. A research studentship at the Wellcome Unit for the History of Medicine at the University of Oxford led her to her doctoral thesis, being published by Routledge as 'The Politics of Nursing Knowledge', 1996. She lectured in the Department of Nursing and Midwifery Studies at the University of Nottingham, and was awarded a Harkness Fellowship to study political leadership in nursing at the University of Pennsylvania with Linda Aiken. She was appointed to the position of Director of the Centre for Policy in Nursing Research at the London School of Hygiene and Tropical Medicine in 1995.

Chapter 1

Veronica Bishop is editor of *Nursing Times Research* and professor of nursing at de Montfort University, Leicester. After undertaking clinical research at the Royal College of Surgeons she joined the Civil Service as a nursing officer, where she had responsibility for a large body of research specifically related to nursing and midwifery. She moved into the Nursing Directorate of the National Health Service Executive (NHSE) in 1992, with the particular remit to develop nursing practice, and initiated the strategic document *Vision for the Future: The Nursing, Midwifery and Health Visiting Contribution to Health and Health Care*. While at the directorate she set up the CNO Practice Advisory Group and developed the DoH Nursing Practice Database for the NHS. Other responsibilities have included being lead nursing officer for clinical supervision, the NDU project and the Delphi practice initiatives. Since leaving the DoH she has continued to work on clinical supervision and on innovations in practice development.

Supervisor's Comments: Emeritus Professor J.P. Payne
OStJ, MB, ChB (Ed), DA, FFARCS, MD (hc) Uppsala, DSc (Med) London, FRCA.

Professor Payne was the British Oxygen Professor of Anaesthetics and Director of the Research Department of Anaesthetics, Royal College of Surgeons, England, and Professor of Anaesthetics at the University of London. He is currently Emeritus Professor, University of London. He has published over 400 papers, mostly on anaesthesia, clinical pharmacology, clinical measurement, metabolic changes in relation to anaesthesia, measurement of neuromuscular block and the uptake, distribution and elimination of alcohol. His miscellaneous papers include contributions to education, organisation and medico-political problems.

Chapter 2

Suzie Page, RGN, BEd(Hons), MSc, is a Senior Lecturer in Research at Thames Valley University and a part-time PhD student. The working title of her PhD (registered in the Department of Human Sciences, Brunel University) is 'Cardiopulmonary Resuscitation: An Anthropological Perspective'.

Chapter 3

Trudy Stevens, SRN, SCM, BA/MA (Cantab), MSc has been a practising midwife for 23 years, ten of which have been spent overseas working in resource-poor countries. She obtained her first degree, in Social Anthropology, from Cambridge University and then her Masters degree in Social Research Methods whilst commencing the study she describes here. She is currently a doctoral student at Thames Valley University.

Supervisor's Comments: Professor Judith Lathlean
Judith is Independent Research Consultant in Health Care, a Visiting Professor at the University of Reading and an Associate Fellow of the Royal College of Nursing Institute's Mental Health Programme. She has many years' experience of undertaking and managing health care and education research and of supervising higher degree students in different universities, especially those doing MPhil/PhD degrees. She is committed to improving standards in higher degree supervision through her own practice and by the provision of training programmes and support for supervisors.

Chapter 4

Owen Barr is a lecturer in Nursing, School of Health Sciences, University of Ulster at Coleraine. He is option leader for the Community Learning Disability Nursing Option within the BSc (Hons) Community Nursing and also has input relating to people with learning disabilities within the BSc (Hons) Nursing and BSc (Hons) Social Work. He is particularly interested in how parents and other family members adapt to having a person with learning disabilities as a family member and has previously written and researched in this area. The focus of his MSc was on the expectations and experiences that parents of children with inherited disabilities have of genetic counselling.

Supervisor's Comments: Robin Millar
Robin is Lecturer in the School of Behavioural and Communication Sciences at the University of Ulster at Magee and the course director of the MSc in Guidance and Counselling. He has an active interest in bereavement counselling and a further involvement in the field of occupational and organisational communication. He acted as the research supervisor for the MSc completed by Owen Barr.

Chapter 5

Dawn Hobson became interested in the application of moral philosophy to ethics in nursing whist studying for her first degree and for qualification as a registered nurse. She received funding to study philosophy for a Master's degree after qualifying, with a view to further investigating its potential application to nursing. Dawn then worked as a staff nurse in the area of learning disabilities and subsequently cancer care for some years, becoming increasingly interested in the provision of palliative care in acute contexts. Her application to study for a PhD was initially an attempt to apply moral philosophy to some of the ethical issues she had witnessed in practice, although the study changed direction in the light of certain discoveries. Dawn is currently writing up the thesis.

Supervisor's Comments: Alfons Grieder
Alfons has for many years been a member of staff at the City University in London and is presently Reader in Philosophy and Head of the Philosophy Division. He studied physics, mathematics and philosophy at the Swiss Federal Institute, Zurich, where he worked as Assistant in Mathematics. He subsequently continued his studies in philosophy of

science and obtained his PhD. Before arriving in this country, and again since the 1970s, modern continental philosophy, especially phenomenology and existential philosophy, has been a main interest of his. He devoted much of his energy to making it better known on this side of the Channel, both in his teaching and research, and also as an active member (and, for a few years, president) of the British Society for Phenomenology.

Supervisor's Comments: Julienne Meyer
Julienne is Professor of Adult Nursing at City University. Her research interests include user and carer involvement, interprofessional working and practice development through action research. She currently leads a team of researchers whose work focuses on the health and social care of older people within a variety of different settings including A&E, primary and secondary care interface, general medicine and rehablitation. She is particularly interested in the value and contribution of nursing, changing roles and the management of change and innovation. At the start of her career she held a variety of clinical roles and later, as a qualified teacher, moved into nurse education. Her current interest in action research draws on her past experience and reflects her firm commitment to improving practice.

Chapter 6

Bill Stein is a graduate of the University of Strathclyde Business School, a Fellow of the Chartered Insurance Institute and a Chartered Insurance Practitioner. He entered the academic world after 18 years in insurance, latterly as liability and property underwriter for a major UK insurer. He has continued to have an interest in conventional 'insurable' risks but has developed an interest in the management of 'risk' in general, particularly in the developing area of healthcare risk management. His work as a lecturer in the Department of Risk and Financial Services at Glasgow Caledonian University involves teaching on undergraduate and postgraduate programmes, consultancy and research in the UK and overseas. He has contributed to several textbooks.

Supervisor's Comments: Professor John Reid
Following an initial career in the insurance industry, John pursued a successful academic career retiring in 1997 as Professor and Head of the Department of Risk and Financial Services at Glasgow Caledonian University. His academic career oversaw a period of major development

for risk management, particularly its development beyond industry and commerce into the new areas of health and public authorities. He has written and lectured extensively on risk management topics, particularly in the specialist areas of health and safety management and risk management in local authorities. John was active in many professional bodies, including the Association of Local Authority Risk Managers (serving on the National Executive Committee); the Association of Insurance and Risk Managers; the Royal Society for the Prevention of Accidents; the Institute of Occupational Safety and Health; and the Institute of Risk Management. He is a graduate of the University of Edinburgh, a Fellow of the Chartered Insurance Institute and a Fellow of the Institute of Risk Management.

Supervisor's Comments: Professor Jennifer Hunt
Jennifer was Director of the Nursing Research Initiative for Scotland before retiring. She has held posts at University College, Cardiff, The London Hospital and the Royal Marsden Hospital, London. She has also held senior management posts and worked in the Department of Health. She has been a member of numerous national committees and working groups including the Standing Nursing and Midwifery Advisory Committee, the Audit Commission, the Clinical Standards Advisory Group, the Acute Healthcare Research Committee and the Scottish Cancer Therapy Network. Her research interests have included pain management, organisational climate, clinical outcomes and utilisation of research findings.

Chapter 7

Maureen Coombs RGN, Dip Nursing (Lond), BSc (Hons), PGDip Ed, MSc Nursing, has developed her career almost entirely within the field of critical care. She has held senior research posts in coronary, cardiothoracic and general intensive care. Her most recent post as senior sister/service delivery unit manager on the adult intensive care unit at the John Radcliffe Hospital, Oxford, allowed her to provide clinical and professional leadership combined with key management responsibilities of service delivery. Having been awarded a competitive scholarship at Oxford Brookes University, she is currently seconded from this role to undertake full time doctoral studies. However, she continues to maintain a clinical practical role on the unit. These studies, due for completion in April 2000, are entitled 'Nursing, medicine and policy development in intensive care – an ethnography to explore the developing role of the nurse'. Maureen is past chair of the British Association of Critical Care Nurses, a role she used to actively foster collaboration between all nursing and medical critical care organisations. She maintains her enthusiasm and commitment to critical care nursing through her publications and national paper presentations.

Supervisor's Comments: Professor Helen Bartlett PhD, MSc, BA, REV, RGN
Helen Bartlett is Deputy Head (Research) in the School of Health Care at Oxford Brookes University and Director of the Oxford Centre for Health Care Research and Development. Prior to joining Oxford Brookes University in 1995, she held research and teaching positions in health sciences, social sciences and nursing in the UK, Australia and Hong Kong. Professor Bartlett has a PhD (1990) and MSc (1983) in Public Policy from the University of Bath and a BA Nursing (1977) from Newcastle upon Tyne Her research interests have focused on aged care policy and provision in the UK, Asia and Australia, in particular the quality of long-term care. Current projects also include the evaluation of primary care and health promotion initiatives. Professor Bartlett is author of three research-based books concerned with the quality of care of older people in residential and nursing homes.

I. Surviving a research degree: a personal view and review of the literature

Author
Veronica Bishop

Commentary
Emeritus Professor J.P. Payne

INTRODUCTION

At the time of writing 16 years have elapsed since I undertook my MPhil and 13 since I completed my PhD. Given such a time span one might assume that 'things had changed' and that the difficulties, strategies and solutions which formed much of my higher education would bear little relevance to today's students. However, I know that this is not the case from the many conversations I have had over the past years – initially in my capacity as a nursing officer in the Research and Development division at the Department of Health and later as a professor of nursing and as editor of *Nursing Times Research*. It was whilst talking with my colleagues on the Board of this research and development journal that the idea arose to 'lift the lid' on many of the dilemmas that postgraduate nurse students in particular face, and to share their experiences in an effort to demystify academia. This is important if those who have not involved themselves in study so far are to be tempted to enter a two-way relationship with academia and to share their ideas and expertise.

I well remember when, as a student nurse, the first degree nurses came on stream. How we nurses in traditional training resented them! And now I know how vulnerable they felt, in the face of our practice-based experience – what a missed opportunity for sharing experiences and for mutual growth.

Whist two decades have passed since then, these misunderstandings of academic isolation and a perceived lack of appreciation of practical 'hands on' skills still exist, and if this book goes some small way to overcome these it has succeeded in its aim.

For those of you who are already involved in academic work the following chapters offer an opportunity to share, in a unique way, the challenges faced by selected authors. These authors are currently carrying out research, either for a Master's degree or for a doctorate and, in collaboration with their academic supervisors, address particular aspects of their research experience to date. I hope that this book will highlight for the potential student those problems which may arise and offer possible solutions. Those already on the road heading for higher degrees will perhaps feel less isolated – a problem shared may not be a problem halved but it is very comforting to know that you are not especially unblessed in your struggles!

In this chapter it is the intention to present issues raised in the small volume of work published on working for research degrees, with the specific aim of giving advice on how to keep the postgraduate student on an even keel in what can be very muddy and turbulent waters. A high percentage of those who register for a higher degree do not complete; success is in large part due to tenacity and the ability to keep a sense of perspective. I hope that this chapter will provide insights which will help the reader to develop both of these assets. The style used is an intentional break from that of formal academia in order to personalise what can be, for some, a very depersonalising experience.

To set the scene, let me state at the outset that I am not a natural academic. I am, in fact, very much a dreamer. I had attended a minor public school, for which my parents paid fees as I had failed the eleven plus and, in spite of passing the entrance exam, my father was convinced until the day that he died that I was only accepted there because they were short of fee-paying pupils! I surprised everyone by managing to pass three 'O' levels, this small success being attributable mainly, I suspect, to the fact that I loved the poem 'The Lady of Shallot' by Tennyson which I knew by heart and which appeared as an exam question in the English paper. The success in English grammar and art I can only put down to kind examiners, neat handwriting and an interesting use of colour. If anyone had suggested at that time that one day I would achieve recognisable academic status they would have been laughed out of court...

I have sketched this brief profile to illustrate that research degrees can be attained by ordinary mortals. Success is not only the province of the exceptionally academically gifted, it is attainable by anyone who is in the position to register for a research degree, has the ongoing support of relevant academic advice and supervision, is blessed with, or able to develop, a generous amount of tenacity and is prepared to embrace critical thinking and hard work. This may sound frivolous, but these really are the essentials needed to successfully complete a research degree and are attributes which the reader will recognise in my co-authors from their accounts of their research degree activities in this book.

SOCIAL AND ACADEMIC OVERVIEW

When I successfully completed my doctorate in the 1980s there were, to my knowledge, only around 20 or so other nurses in the UK with a similar qualification. Today the Steinberg Collection at the Royal College of Nursing holds the theses of around 185 successful PhDs, a significant increase and one discussed more fully in terms of ascertaining current strengths and weaknesses in the research capacity within nursing, midwifery and health visiting by Rafferty and Traynor (1997).

Why this increase? There are several reasons. Nursing as it is developing today has many of its origins in the reforms of Florence Nightingale which were based on meticulous investigations, yet Simpson (1971) and later Salvage (1998) note how this same problem-solving approach was not passed on as part of the Nightingale tradition. Indeed it could be said that Nightingale encouraged a hierarchical system in nursing which regarded nurse training as a character-forming process rather than an education for the development of a scientific knowledge base. This was to change later in the development of nursing as a true profession, and the emergence of research in nursing may be attributed, in part, to the changing role of women in society after the Second World War. Women began to take a more prominent role in the labour market and gradually accrued some political strength. Increased opportunities in general, higher education and quite rapid advances in medical science and its applied technology to patients demanded commensurate changes in nursing practice (Lelean, 1980). None the less, changes in nurse education in the UK were slow to follow changing patterns in society and, while the universities of Edinburgh and Manchesterbroke with tradition and commenced degree courses for nurses in the 1960s (mirroring the USA who had developed graduate programmes for nurses since the 1920s), those who passed through these portals were seen by many in the nursing professions as an elite and far removed from the norm.

In 1972 a government committee set up to consider the nursing professions published its report (Briggs Report, 1972) which stated that nursing should be a 'research-based profession'. This heralded a slow but accumulative development in research initiatives, mainly, though not exclusively, within universities and the Royal College of Nursing, fostered by nurses within the Department of Health.

The term 'research' was added on to many middle or senior nurse job titles in the NHS, often with little or no thought as to what experience or support structures were required to enable the post-holder to function in research terms. Despite this often superficial approach to nursing research, sufficient studies of high quality developed over the years to make its mark on health care delivery and for the emergence of a new debate – that of the nursing research contribution to multidisciplinary studies. The Department of Health, in an attempt to develop a cohesive strategy for research and development in nursing and midwifery, convened a task force (Department of Health, 1993) which would facilitate increased activity in quality nursing research and enhance nurses' and midwives' research expertise. At the time of writing (April 1999) a part-time post of professor of nursing research at the Department of Health has been created and nursing research is now intended to be largely incorporated within the broader research and development (R&D) NHS programme.

In parallel with the activities described above was a move for a greater degree of empowerment and autonomy in the nursing and midwifery professions which demanded universally held educational standards, rather than the traditional apprenticeship model of learning which had scant academic recognition. September 1989 saw the introduction of Project 2000, a diploma or degree-based education programme for nurses (Jowett, Walton and Payne, 1994) which speeded up the profession's engagement with research, though not necessarily for the best of reasons or supported by sound structures. Higher education carries with it the expectation of significant research activity from its teachers and from its students, as the educational institutions are mainly funded through central government selected bodies whose criteria for allocating funds depend on peer review and student numbers. Peer-review, in this instance, is judged largely by publications in respected, reviewed academic journals and by external funding obtained from commissioned research. The move into higher education and the concomitant need of these institutions to vie for central funding through numbers of students and research activity has resulted in a professional turbulence which is still ongoing.

Within this turbulence Kitson describes the lack of unity within the nursing profession on its central image and the tensions between the scientific skills of nursing and the core values of professional caring (Kitson, 1996). Mirrored in this discussion is the question of what contribution academia should make to practice and the issue of clinical credibility of nurse teachers and professors and the links between academia and practice. Academia and nursing are relatively new companions (Maggs, 1996) and the merits or otherwise of such a relationship are a constant source of discussion between professional leaders and those practising 'hands on' care. This begs the question of what areas of research a nurse academic might most beneficially pursue – an important issue which is discussed more fully in the section on choosing an area to study. The process of attaining a PhD may not be via a conventional nursing career track – indeed, my own academic career followed a very medically dominated path. It was only through my determination to bridge the opportunities offered through multidisciplinary work with nursing issues that I was able to contribute to the professional agenda in later years. There are many opportunities to be grasped through multidisciplinary working, though a novice researcher may find it difficult to establish a personal focus and avoid being swept along on a tide of data collection which, while important, does not perhaps allow for the intrinsic nursing input. An example of where multidisciplinary working has been very successful is discussed more fully in Chapter 4.

With the NHS culture broadening, albeit slowly, to take on board the concept of research which goes beyond the medical model, it is now somewhat easier for a nurse to apply to undertake research, particularly on a part-time basis, than used to be the case, though obtaining the necessary funding may not be so easy (see Chapter 2). It is this gradual change in culture which has enabled nurses to extend their traditional role of caring without questioning to one described by Hancock (1996) as one of meeting the challenges of providing health care. She sees this as being achieved by nurses increasingly using existing research and by undertaking new studies to prove that nursing interventions contribute to quality care, and sees nursing research as 'revealing the extra dimension that nursing brings to the health care team'.

The social and professional changes briefly described above explain, in part, the increased research activity by nurses. These changes are in health care delivery, the move into higher education, the interest in research initiated by diploma or undergraduate studies, the need, in terms of career options, to widen the scope of professional practice and to underpin the art of nursing with science. All this was set against the ever-increasing drive for cost-effectiveness. These selected historical events are provided in order that the reader may place themselves in a social as well as a professional context when considering their potential in studying for a research degree.

RESEARCH DEGREE APPROACHES: MOTIVATION

Despite this upturn in interest (or professional pragmatism) in relation to research, it is clear from many conversations with nurse colleagues that research is regarded as a mysterious and somewhat esoteric process which may well be out of reach. Salvage, in considering the mixed motives of evidence-based practice, suggests that the idea of research and all it seems to represent is seductive (Salvage, 1998). Seduction, where this may be the case, is usually short-lived as it appears that there are a number of us who arrive at the decision to study for research degrees with little background or confidence that it may be an area where success can be achieved. Howard and Sharp (1983) write that most people associate the word 'research' with activities which are substantially removed from day-to-day life and which are pursued by outstandingly gifted persons with an unusual level of commitment. They go on to state that 'there is, of course, a good deal of truth in this viewpoint but we could argue that the pursuit is not restricted to this type of person and indeed may prove to be a stimulating and satisfying experience for many people with a trained and enquiring mind'. Neither viewpoint is necessarily true. The purpose of a PhD is to train the mind!

Reasons for undertaking a higher degree will vary with each individual. Given the total number of home domiciled post-graduate students in the UK across all subjects (over 239,900 full- and part-time postgraduate students in 1997, Higher Education Statistics Agency press release, Table 1. p 22), the task of identifying what motivates those who undertake research studies may have been perceived as too vast. Aspirations, though, are in many instances borne of similar human characteristics and, judging by accumulated anecdotal evidence, I think that there is shared benefit in exposing some of these, particularly given this particular time in the history of professional nursing. My particular motivation was bedded in a deep-seated but very rational embarrassment at my lack of formal qualifications. After five years of working in a clinical research department, observing and sometimes helping post graduates with their work, I asked if I could – with my very limited academic background – register to undertake an MPhil. Thanks to the support of my head of department and to the 'open door' policy of the now disbanded Council for National Academic Awards (CNAA), I was accepted as an MPhil student following approval of my detailed proposed plan of work. I was both excited and frightened by the prospect of what, for me, was a greater achievement than I had ever believed possible. I was to research the clinical application of non-invasive monitoring equipment in anaesthesia and intensive care – the clinical specialties in which I had most experience and which were complementary to work I was currently undertaking in the anaesthetic research department of the Royal College of Surgeons. The study was intentionally broad based, to compensate for the lack of a first degree, and involved in depth aspects of physiology which did not come easily to me. However, one aspect which I did really come to grips with, and take forward in a very innovative way, was the quantification of emotional stress, and it was this aspect of my work which particularly appealed to my examiners at my viva and to the examining board of the CNAA. They recommended that I should take that work forward through a PhD, and I shall always be grateful for that encouragement. Full of the energy born of success I immediately registered with London University to undertake a PhD. My motives were mixed – I was excited by the prospect of developing the work I had started, but I was also conscious of changing perceptions about myself. For those readers who have achieved a first degree the mental leap from there to PhD may not present such a stretch of the imagination as it did for me with my background of three 'O' levels! Perhaps most importantly in terms of motivation, I had begun to be involved with the politics of nursing, albeit in a small way, and recognised that I was unlikely to contribute to or to change anything in nursing unless I had some authority or knowledge which would be held in esteem by those I wanted to be in dialogue with.

Here then is the nub – without motivation the student is unlikely to complete their studies, or produce work of a high enough standard. Before embarking on a research degree, first be sure that it is what is wanted. This may seem a rather foolish statement, but if the student does not have a real interest in the research and has little clear view as to the relevance of the work to their career, then the motivation will be missing. Whatever the reason for undertaking a research degree, whether it is to prove something at a personal level, to change practice, to alter thinking or to improve career options, motivation is the key to success and ways may need to be devised to keep it from lagging. Philips and Pugh (1987) highlight the need to understand the nature of a research degree, particularly a PhD. Many students overestimate what is required and become very despondent. The phrase which my supervisor used to utter to his many students when they were in despair was: 'You are not aiming for the Nobel prize.' Remember, a PhD degree simply establishes that the candidate is capable of doing research.

CHOOSING THE AREA OF STUDY

When I left the Royal College of Surgeons one of my leaving presents was a book entitled *The Drunken Goldfish* (Harston, 1987). This wonderfully irreverent book is the result of a collection by the author of published research which is, as far as one is able to judge, of little use to mankind. For example, were you aware that research has established that rats are more attracted to other rats than to tennis balls, that holy water does not affect the growth of radishes and that the effects of alcohol on goldfish to remember things has been investigated? Unless the researcher has a bank balance which precludes the need to relate the area of study to the society in which he or she works, it is good sense to choose an area of study which will benefit the employer/environment/funding agency. The logic of this is not just one of funding sensibilities. The likelihood of a research student completing their studies in a reasonable time is far greater if they are working in that area – the work will enrich their research and the research may benefit their work. This is one of the most powerful ways of bridging the oft-quoted and very serious 'theory–practice gap' (Bishop, 1996) which is discussed more fully in Chapter 7. Many postgraduate students have struggled to complete their research years after they had hoped to finish, because the subject matter is not complementary to their daily lives and there are only 24 hours in the day. If I had not selected subjects for my theses which wove easily into my work as an anaesthetic research sister I am sure that I would never have completed the first, let alone the second. This view is supported by Rudestam and Newton (1992) who describe the selection of an appropriate topic as the first major challenge in conducting research, and they emphasise the usefulness of working with others who are interested in linked areas of study. Sustaining interest and essential motivation over some years is far easier when the student is part of a group which shares an interest, a critical mass who can act as peer support and provide useful critique. Very few students thrive in isolation and those studying through open learning techniques have to devise ways to overcome this.

Having selected a subject to research, the refining of the actual research question can be quite daunting. Francis (1997) writes: 'the struggle for focus should not be underestimated. It is not easy to combine a good research topic with originality and with a scope which is contained sufficiently to be a feasible enterprise for a doctorate' Bell (1987) highlights the need, once the topic to be studied has been selected, to decide on the precise focus of the study, an activity which Rudestam and Newton (1992) have noticed many students have difficulty with – the transformation of an interesting idea into a researchable question. It has certainly been my experience, when talking with newly engaged researchers and experienced ones alike, that teasing out the essence of a study and translating that into a research question which is manageable is no easy task and requires a great deal of time and consultation. It is not a matter to be rushed, for time spent here will pay dividends later. Read up on the subject, carry out a literature search and pull out those papers which complement the area of particular interest. Bell (1987) suggests that it is helpful to draw up a list of 'first thoughts' and to formulate some research questions, no matter how vague they may seem. Lawton (1997) suggests that the main points of manageability are checked by asking the following questions:

- Is it a feasible topic?

- Is there enough in it for the required thesis?

- Am I proposing to collect too much data?

- What about the methodology?

Once the research question has been isolated from the area of interest the method of inquiry needs to be identified, and there are many published guides available to the reader including Abbot and Sapsford (1998), Graves and Varma (1997), Rudestam and Newton (1992), Polgar and Thomas (1991), Bell (1987), Morse and Field (1995), Fox (1982), to name but a few. Morse and Field, in their revised edition of *Nursing Research* (1995), note the acceptability of qualitative methods today, compared with their first edition in 1985, and the ease with which they can now choose examples to quote from. It is not in the remit of this book to describe either quantitative or qualitative approaches to research nor to add to the perennial debate as to the value of one over the other (Avis and Robinson, 1996). Suffice to say that the pursuit of scientific knowledge is dependent on a commitment to systematically obtained evidence and logical argument, whichever methodology is employed. It is, however, our aim to identify problem areas which can, with care, be avoided. Whichever methodology is selected – and the following chapters offer the reader some insight into why each author selected their chosen way – either the study is structured by the research question, or the study structures the research. As Rudestam and Newton point out (1992) there are dangers in the latter approach, even for the more experienced researcher, of ending up with massive quantities of data and no idea of what to do with them. It is too easy for the novice researcher (and for those who are more experienced) to lay themselves open to the need to collect massive data sets which may, in the final analysis, prove unhelpful. On the other hand, particularly, when the public is involved in a study, one cannot go back and collect new information – the opportunity is lost. So a fine balance between needs to be kept what information is needed to reach an answer to the research question selected, which variables may impact on that and which data will muddy the waters. It is a cry common to statisticians that researchers call upon their expertise too late in the game, thus adding tremendously to the stresses of carrying out a successful research project. Identify a willing statistician early in the study design deliberations, don't be afraid of the fact that they appear to speak another language, press on and tell them what the study is about, its aims and objectives and what kind of information is thought to be obtainable. They will, in most cases, reward this involvement ten-fold, not only in the research design but also in assisting in the analyses. This collaboration will also pay dividends when the research proposal is submitted to any ethics or research committee.

There are important ethical dimensions to data collection and these are discussed more fully in Chapter 3. The submission of any research proposal or project to the local ethics committees is not only good practice and legally wise but also affords the opportunity for further input from experts. While the focus of many of these experts may be singularly unidisciplinary and not without difficulties (Glenister, 1996; Neuberger, 1996) it is important to realise that you cannot function in isolation, and goodwill, as well as legal cover, is essential to the success of any research study.

SELECTING A SUPERVISOR

The role of the supervisor and their importance to the success or otherwise of a fruitful research degree cannot be over-emphasised, a view strongly held by other authors (Lawton, 1997; Philips and Pugh, 1987). In the following chapters the role of the supervisor is discussed in very individualistic ways by each of the writers – and the supervisors themselves provide comment. Sometimes this very important relationship is taken for granted and the inherent expectations are not voiced and indeed may not be shared. This may result in an almost cursory exchange which brings little to what could and should be an enriching process for both parties. Styles of supervision will vary of course, but I remember vividly one of the supervisors in the department where I worked during my academic studies. His mode of supervision, which generally induced very high motivation in his students, was extremely prescriptive in nature and involved a certain amount of shouting which, when focused on the female students, often resulted in tears at his early morning tutorials. His success rate for completed PhDs and MPhils was high and none that I am aware of failed. However, it was not a style which is acceptable to everyone and certainly not one in which I could have developed academic confidence! It may well suit the student to have more than one supervisor. The subject which I chose to study for my PhD could have bypassed the interests of my profession – nursing – so I took care to involve a second supervisor, a nurse academic, to complement the skills of my medically qualified first supervisor. Professor Wilson-Barnett kindly agreed to take on this role, and helped me to maintain my nursing focus. This worked well, and I think that it was this conscious decision to keep bridging the gap between the professions and to link my work with both my paymaster and nursing which has opened exciting career doors for me since. Any supervisor must fully understand the nature of higher degrees and understand that even adult students can be childlike in their need for support and discipline. While my supervisor was more inclined to leave his students to motivate themselves, he was never slow in returning fully commented reports upon drafted work and was always available for discussion or advice. Relationships between supervisors and students will be as variable as those involved in them, but there is, I think, one constant for a good supervisory relationship, and that is trust – trust that the supervisor believes in the student, that however foolish the student feels, or may sometimes appear, he or she has the ability to win. Indeed, if it were not for the stalwart belief of my supervisor in my ability I would never have considered the academic journey, and without his tolerance and support I certainly would never have completed it.

It may not be within the gift of the organisation where the student is registered to allow a choice of supervisor, or the one of preference may already have too many students, as highlighted by Graves (1997) who identifies the languishing of many part-time students to be attributable to overloaded supervisors. What *is* within the gift of the student is the ability to involve other willing and appropriate internal or external academics, as long as this is done in an open and professional manner. The spirit of critique is pivotal to the development of research and practice (Bishop, 1998) but is not, as yet, an established part of the nursing culture. Criticism without support is likely to be very destructive, but structured critique can only be beneficial to both the student and the critic. Importantly, familiarity with a critical culture is half-way to overcoming the possible terror of a viva! But it is not just the support of a sound supervisor that is needed, though little will be accomplished comfortably without this – the love and understanding of friends and family are also important and those heartfelt acknowledgements at the front of most theses are testimony to this.

KNOW THE SYSTEM: GETTING ORGANISED

Before starting on the higher academic road it is essential to have a route map – in other words find out all you can about the organisation(s) with which you wish to study, their particular rules and regulations in terms of setting out proposals, style, and timings for submission of theses; what Philips and Pugh (1987) describe as 'getting into the system'. Do not rely on hearsay, however authoritative it may seem to be – organisations change their rules and regulations from time to time. Ignorance of these facts will not soften the administrative face of academia when the student who has run out of time and not re-registered turns out to have followed the preferred format of another institution, or failed in any other bureaucratic necessities! On the contrary it may be interpreted as arrogance. Funding is discussed in Chapter 2 in some detail. Sufficient to note here that securing funding for a limited time in the hope that further funding will be found later may prove to be disastrous; changes in employment terms and conditions may preclude the student from completing their research studies. I have known some excellent researchers unable to complete their studies owing to lack of adequate funding or to short-term employment contracts which may not be renewed. It is also essential to try to adhere to a set timetable, albeit a flexible one. Francis (1997) supports this view and maintains that a personal plan of work with an agreed timetable is necessary if activity is to be maintained. This is central to the success of any research and flows from understanding the system and planning your timetable according to your needs and those of the organisations with which you are involved. Salmon (1992), in describing ten selected students' experiences, takes a far more relaxed view and states that everyone has to find within themselves ways of working and sees the creative process as a notoriously capricious activity. While I would agree that creativity is rarely a mechanical process which can be turned on and off at will, I would caution against awaiting a visitation of the Muses – some self-discipline is usually necessary to prompt the creative process. In the first year most postgraduates run with the notion that there is plenty of time, and I recall a poem pinned to our notice board which commenced with 'He had a year to do it in…' and ended with the subject rushing to achieve in minutes what needed months. A classic syndrome is that of sharpening pencils or tidying the study area – anything rather than putting pen to paper or finger to word processor! May (1997) and Bell (1987) stress the need to be organised and on time in undertaking research and the value of deadlines agreed with supervisors; these are not only useful for the student but also help keep the supervisor in touch.

INTROSPECTION VERSUS SANITY

A genius, a research student with unlimited funding and thus no anxiety as to the duration of his or her work, or a total optimist may avoid the dangers of introspection; the rest of us may easily fall prey to them and suffer tunnel vision, a state of mind unlikely to improve any study. I recall a close friend ringing me at home during the period of statistical analyses of my PhD data.

'How are you?' she asked, with gentle concern for a single parent of a year-old baby and aware of the long hours that I was working.

'My correlation is poor,' I wailed. She sharply pointed out that she was not interested in my correlation, significant or otherwise. How was the baby, was my cold better, was I in the real world? Frankly, I was not; my data and I had developed a terrible symbiosis and I was in danger of disappearing into my next 'T' test! Such introspection is not necessarily the province of single parents or isolated scholars, nor is it age related. The need to keep a balanced view of life through personal and professional links cannot be underestimated, particularly once the first flush of enthusiasm has waned. When I was nursing in a very busy cardio-thoracic unit in the 1970s, at a time when patients with very poor prognoses were operated on (with the concomitant depressing results), I used to compensate for this unbalanced view of life, or rather the demise of it, by partying as if it would go out of fashion. Oddly, I can't remember what mechanisms I used during my six years of postgraduate study. Perhaps my son provided an anchor – there is nothing like a pile of nappies to refocus the mind from the esoteric on to the norm.

After the first flush of enthusiasm it is easy to lose heart, progress seems to be slow, and there is often little to show for hours of concentration. Windows of opportunity to collect data may be wiped out by someone falling sick, by increased workload outside the specific area of study, or by mechanical failures. This is all part of the higher degree process and anyone who does not suffer any or all of these trials and more is truly privileged.

The period half-way through the research has been identified as the time when postgraduates get 'stuck' and feel that they are getting nowhere (Philips and Pugh, 1987; Hudderson, 1977). Some of this dissatisfaction may be due to the disappointment described by Francis (1997) in the reduction of the scope of the work in order that the project remains manageable. Conversely, if the project has not been managed as well as it might and the initial idea has run out of control, the researcher may be drowning under a sea of data sets. In this situation some very clear thinking needs to be employed as to the way ahead. Has this occurred because of poor supervision, poor acceptance of advice or inadequate piloting? Should the research question be modified in the light of the available data in a manner which will be acceptable to the examining board? Can the dilemma be turned into an advantage? Usually it can, given careful thinking and the will to succeed.

As the work progresses so too does the student's independence, a fact noted by Philips and Pugh (1987), and this was certainly my personal experience. What is very helpful, both in personal and in career terms, is to publish work in progress. Research journals vary in their appreciation of unfinished work, but it is my strongly held view, which as editor of *Nursing Times Research* I am able to exercise, that well-documented research in progress offers a great deal to both the researcher and the academic community. It has the advantages of avoiding the pitfalls of tunnel vision and egocentricity, while encouraging critical debate on a given subject.

Whether the student publishes or not, it is of vital importance that copies are kept of every written word. It is unwise to place all trust in a computer – it can crash. Keep a disk elsewhere. The story of the research student who lost all copies of his thesis in a fire is too awful to contemplate; keep a spare copy or disk in another place. Careful documentation of references and good record keeping will pay enormous dividends later, when the gritty cross-referencing has to be completed. Rest assured that the reference which one was sure one would never forget will slip the mind.

In my attempt to identify some of the difficulties of doing a research degree and suggesting ways to overcome these, I have perhaps neglected to highlight the enormous sense of joy and accomplishment that accompanies successful completion. Education of any kind offers choices which were possibly hitherto unlikely and extending formal education to undertaking a research degree can only increase the student's view of their world and their choices within it. It is not the wish or option for many to undertake research and there is always a cost in following an unorthodox path, or in breaking new ones. This is something which has to be faced when considering studying for a higher degree. The questions must be asked 'Do I really need it? There are many other challenges, is this the one for me?' before tying up a life for a number of years. Do I have any regrets? Of course a few, not least that I did not have access to a book like this at the beginning of my journey. No single book will exactly cover all possible situations but sharing experiences with other nurses would have been particularly helpful.

Supervisor's Comments
Emeritus Professor J.P. Payne

It is perhaps fitting that Veronica obtained her doctorate in a department of anaesthetics since there are close parallels in the development of academic nursing with academic anaesthesia and more or less for the same reasons. Accordingly, it is appropriate that I should devote some space to the recent historical development of both disciplines.

The first academic appointment in anaesthesia in the UK, and probably anywhere in the world, was made at the University of Edinburgh in 1902 (Mason, 1988), and a further appointment was made the University of Manchester in the early 1920s. It is surely no coincidence that the same universities were in the forefront of graduate education for nurses, albeit at a much later date.

Despite these appointments in anaesthesia there was no great pressure to establish a university chair in the subject until Lord Nuffield funded the Nuffield chair of anaesthetics at the University of Oxford in 1987 with Dr (later Sir Robert) Macintosh as the first professor (Bryce-Smith et al, 1963) Even then, without Lord Nuffield's insistence it is unlikely that the Oxford chair of anaesthetics would ever have been instituted.

The real academic developments in anaesthesia and in nursing had to wait until after the introduction of the National Health Service in 1948. In fulfilment of the undertaking given by the wartime coalition government that when the war was ended, health care would be provided free at the point of delivery for all the people of the UK, the first post-war government introduced the National Health Service Act (HMSO, 1946) which was brought into effect in July 1948.

Medicine was never to be the same again. Despite the lack of enthusiasm of many senior doctors and the implacable opposition of a few others, younger doctors, particularly those who had served in the Armed Forces, were prepared to co-operate with the government and did so wholeheartedly, and there was a general air of optimism for the future shared by the great majority of people.

Of all the specialties, anaesthesia was to benefit most by the introduction of a more rational system of health care and an integrated salaried service for hospital doctors. Anaesthetists were no longer dependent on the goodwill of surgeons for their income, and the coincident introduction of more effective drugs and the development of more precise and sophisticated anaesthetic techniques began to attract ambitious young doctors who realised that they could build careers for themselves, independent of surgical patronage.

This independence was reinforced by the establishment of a Faculty of Anaesthetists within the Royal College of Surgeons of England, which coincided with the inauguration of the NHS in 1948. With the formation of the Faculty it was further proposed that a department of anaesthetics should be created in the Royal College of Surgeons on the basis that such a department could not fail to give a new impetus to anaesthesia in the United Kingdom. To emphasise the point the new department was to be called the research department of anaesthetics and unlike any at that time (or more recently created university departments), it would be free from formal teaching and administrative commitments. This was accepted and financial support for the new department came largely from covenants made by the elected Fellows of the Faculty – probably a reflection of the enthusiasm and forward thinking of our original Fellows. Nevertheless it became clear that more financial support would be needed if the department was to expand, and shortly after its official opening in July 1957 a chair of anaesthesia was created and endowed by the British Oxygen Company (BOC) which became effective in 1959. Its impact was immediate and it is to the credit of the Department of Health that it had recognised that in a shortage speciality new recruits would go where the *career* prospects were best. A decision was therefore taken to fund chairs of anaesthesia in those health regions where the shortage was most acute, in an attempt to redress the deficit. Subsequently a similar priority was developed in relation to nursing but with less success, possibly because Academe was not then seen by the rank and file of the nursing profession to have any impact on their daily problems (Payne, 1987). The need to develop practice based on sound academic principles which has been recognised and accepted in anaesthesia pertains to nursing, and Veronica sought to achieve this in her studies and in her subsequent career.

When I became director and professor at the department in 1963 I continued to pursue the multidisciplinary approach to research already established by my predecessor, whose staff consisted of a clinical physiologist, a physicist and an anaesthetist, supported by electronics, engineering and mechanical as well as laboratory assistants. I saw the need, however, to change the emphasis from laboratory to clinical research; thus there was a need for clinical access and this was eventually negotiated with the adjacent postgraduate urological hospitals and the associated Institute of Urology, a relationship which proved highly beneficial for all the parties concerned.

With the development of a clinical research programme it became apparent that the clinical investigators would need the assistance of a nurse familiar with invasive techniques of monitoring and capable of supervising the use of mechanical ventilators. It was decided that the nurse should also be a member of the research department and not a member of the hospital staff. There were a number of reasons for this, not least a major ethical issue: most of our research was dependent on the willingness of our patients to participate in the studies and I learnt early that none of the patients refused me if I sought their co-operation – the title professor was still highly regarded at that time! Accordingly it became my practice to allow the junior staff to oversee the patients' permission for our studies accompanied by a knowledgeable nurse.

As director and supervisor to many postgraduate students I held dear the concept of providing an environment which was conducive to shared learning. While training is useful in our society it is already accepted that higher education is a better way forward. Indeed today, according to one author, the average income for women with degrees is 39% higher than for those workers without, while unemployment levels are halved (Philip, 1999). Scholarship in our department was a shared enterprise among the staff, representing as they did a substantial number of disciplines as well as a multiplicity of nationalities and it is not surprising that even those non-graduates, like Veronica, who joined the department with no academic ambitions reconsidered their position. As staff numbers increased, formal weekly staff meetings provided a sympathetic but highly critical audience. In the department all staff were expected to be members of their specialist associations. In Veronica's case there was no nursing association to meet her needs but she was accepted as a member of the Anaesthetic Research Society, which was open to those in whatever discipline who were engaged in anaesthetic research, and she had presented a paper on her work which was accepted in peer review. Although the department had no funds specifically allocated for attendance at meetings the full time anaesthetists on the staff earned substantial fees from private patients in the hospitals and it was agreed amongst them that this money should be used as a research and educational fund for the purpose of supporting attendance at conferences for junior staff, providing certain books and journals and for purchasing equipment not available from other sources. What the department could and did do was to provide technical assistance, standard equipment and access to libraries. In addition, computer facilities were readily available at a time when few departments had such access. Moreover the multidisciplinary nature of the department ensured that advice on almost any subject from anatomy to statistics was readily available, either directly or by reference elsewhere. Above all the department provided an ambience that was conducive to good research and which was generated by the enthusiasm of the research workers themselves as exemplified by Veronica and her subsequent academic progress.

This was the situation in the department when Veronica joined it. She had begun her nurse training after a variety of occupations which had offered her no career prospects but converted her into a mature student even though not much older than her contemporaries in training. After completing it she gained experience in intensive care and in psychiatric nursing, both of which probably made it easier to adjust to the culture shock which she was to encounter in our research programme. However, she was old enough to have developed a maturity which made her acceptable to the senior nursing staff in the hospitals where we carried out our studies, while at the same time young enough to become friends with the various postgraduates with whom she worked. As postgraduate students came and went Veronica gradually became the anchor-woman to whom new members of staff turned for advice and guidance.

Surrounded as she was by a group of ambitious young graduates of both sexes seeking higher diplomas or MPhil, PhD or MD degrees it must have eventually registered with her that intellectually, if not educationally, she was the equal of many. This was probably the spur that led her to approach me somewhat diffidently to ask if there as any way in which she could acquire a degree. Within the department we had a policy that anyone who sought a degree should be encouraged in every way possible. As her potential supervisor I was satisfied that she had the determination and perseverance to do whatever she set out to accomplish and it was a matter of finding the best approach. Her obvious difficulty was her poor school record, no 'A' levels and only 3 'O' levels, none of which was in the sciences. On the basis of her nursing qualification and her work over five years in an academic research department where she had strong support, she was accepted for a MPhil under the aegis of the Council for National Academic Awards. To compensate for her lack of academic study to date I was somewhat prescriptive in that I ensured that this was a very broad-based study which would satisfy any critics. In 1983 she satisfied her examiners with a thesis entitled 'The Application of Non-invasive Measurement Techniques to Anaesthetic Practice and Research', with the added recommendation that she should continue her studies with a doctorate as her objective.

As a member of staff of a department associated with London University Veronica was entitled to register as a PhD student, which she did. Understandably she was anxious to include a nursing component, which I supported as long as the necessary expertise was ensured, and to this end a second supervisor with specialist knowledge in the field of nursing was agreed, Professor Wilson-Barnett. This was a good arrangement. I was available more or less on a daily basis, essentially as a facilitator and Professor Wilson-Barnett guided the candidate on the more specialised aspects of the study.

Modes of supervision vary to suit the individual student and in Veronica's case there was never any need to chase her for work, despite the fact that she was working as a team member in studies unrelated to her own. I took pride in being available to all my staff, working an 'open door' policy, but not everyone took advantage of that. The supervisory relationship has to be two-way and cannot be dependent on either person involved alone. Despite or because of the multiplicity of disciplines and nationalities I like to think that on balance relationships in the department were relatively easy and that there was no strong hierarchical pattern, although there may be those who would contradict me! As director and research supervisor I saw my task as that of a facilitator, adviser and guide rather than critic. Certainly I had my student failures, though they were very few in an overall substantial number, and they were totally predictable in that they lacked real motivation and the ability to accommodate criticism from their peers or even from their supervisors. What I have learnt in my academic career, which has extended over 50 years, is that for a research career the motivation must come from within the individual and it cannot be achieved on the basis of an eight-hour day and a five-day week. And I guess that was one of the other lessons that Veronica learnt at which she has hinted but left unsaid.

REFERENCES

Abbott, P., Sapsford, R. (1998) *Research Methods for Nurses and the Caring Professions.* 2nd edn. Buckingham, Philadelphia: Open University Press.
Avis, M., Robinson, J. (1996) Guest editorial: Continuing Dilemmas in Health Care Research. *Nursing Times Research*; 1: 3.
Bell, J. (1987) *Doing Your Research Project.* Buckingham, Philadelphia: Open University Press.
Bishop, V. (1998) *Clinical Supervision in Practice: Some Questions, Answers and Guidelines.* London: Macmillan/NT Research.

Bishop, V. (1996) *Nursing Times Research;* 1: 1, editorial, 7.

Bishop, V.A. (1999) A personal view of surviving a research degree. In: *Working Towards a Research Degree: Insights from the Nursing Perspective.* London: NT Books.

Bryce-Smith, R., Mitchell, J.V., Parkhouse, J. (1963) *The Nuffield Department of Anaesthetics. Oxford 1937-1962.* Oxford: Oxford University Press.

Department of Health and Social Security (1972) *Report of the Committee on Nursing (Briggs Report).* London: HMSO.

Department of Health (1993) *Report of the Taskforce on a Strategy for Research in Nursing, Midwifery and Health Visiting.* London: Department of Health.

Fox, D.J. (1982) *Fundamentals of Research in Nursing.* Connecticut: Appleton-Century-Crofts.

Francis, H. (1997) The research process. In: Graves, N., Varia, V. (eds) *Working for a Doctorate.* London and New York: Routledge.

Glenister, D. (1996) Nursing Research Ethics: Some problems and recommended changes. *Nursing Times Research;* 1: 3, 184 –190.

Graves, N. (1997) Problems of supervision. In: Graves, N., Varia, V. (eds) *Working for a Doctorate.* London and New York: Routledge.

Hancock, C. (1996) Guest editor. Advanced nursing roles will enhance patient care. *Nursing Times Research;* 1: 2, 93.

Harston, W. (1987) *The Drunken Goldfish.* London: Unwin Hyman.

Higher Education Statistics Agency (1998) press release April 28; 1998. Table 1.

Howard, K., Sharp, J.A. (1983) *The Management of a Student Research Project.* Aldershot: Gower.

Jowett, S., Walton, I., Payne, S. (1994) *Challenges and Change in Nurse Education: A Study of the Implementation of Project 2000.* Slough: National Foundation for Educational Research.

Kitson, A.L. (1996) Does nursing have a future? *British Medical Journal;* 313: 1647–1651.

Lawton, D. (1997) How to succeed in postgraduate study. In: Graves, N., Varia, V. (eds) *Working for a Doctorate.* London and New York: Routledge.

Lelean, S.R. (1980) *Nursing Times.* Occasional papers. Vol 76. no.2. Research in nursing: an overview of DHSS initiatives in developing research in nursing. 1 Jan: 17.

Maggs, C. (1996) Professors of nursing as clinicians and academics: is this the way forward? *Nursing Times Research;* 1: 2, 157–158.

Masson, A.H.B. (1988) The appointment of an anaesthetist. *Anaesthesia;* 43: 146–149.

May, D. (1997) Planning Time. In: Graves, N., Varia, V. (eds) *Working for a Doctorate.* London and New York: Routledge.

Morse, J.M., Field, P.A. (1995) *Nursing Research.* London: Chapman and Hall.

HMSO (1946) National Health Service Act. 1946. London: HMSO.

Neuberger, J. (1996) Commentary. The place of nurses on local research ethics committees. *Nursing Times Research;* 1: 3, 191–192.

Payne, J.P. (1987) Credibility gap. *Nursing Standard;* 10: October, 36–37.

Philip, A. (1999) The benefits of learning. *Guardian;* Feb. 17, 8–9.

Philips, E.M., Pugh, D.S. (1987) *How to Get a PhD.* Milton Keynes, Philadelphia: Open University Press.

Polgar, S., Thomas, S.A. (1991) *Introduction to Research in the Health Sciences.* London, New York: Churchill Livingstone.

Rafferty, A.M., Traynor, M. (1997) Quality and quantity in research policy for nursing. *Nursing Times Research;* 2: 1, 16–27.

Rudestam, K.E., Newton, R. (1992) *Surviving Your Dissertation.* London, New Delhi: Sage Publications Inc.

Salmon, P. (1992) *Achieving a PhD: Ten Students' Experience.* Stoke on Trent: Trentham.

Salvage, J. (1998) Evidence-based practice: a mixture of motives? *Nursing Times Research;* 3: 6.

Simpson, H.M. (1971) Research in nursing: the first step. *Nursing Mirror;* 132: 11, 22–27.

2. Research funding for nurses

Author

Suzie Page

INTRODUCTION

The nuts and bolts of how to write a good research proposal are standard fodder in much of the research methods literature and are often linked to tips on accessing research grants. Moreover, the implications for nursing research of the recent high profile of R&D in the NHS have been reflected in literature (for example, McMahon, 1997) and it is now fairly common to encounter books or articles on how to do research, how to get funding and so forth (for example, Tarling and Crofts, 1998). The intention of this chapter is not to duplicate this information but to focus on the issue of research funding as it pertains to nurses wishing to undertake PhDs. It is perhaps surprising that whilst the need for more nurses educated to doctorate level has been appreciated for some time, particularly by those working in university departments, useful information on the pragmatics involved appears, at best, somewhat dispersed. It could be that the time-consuming activity of locating the information and completing the requisite forms is part of the rite of passage. This chapter is intended to make a small contribution towards easing the process.

A useful starting point to this discussion is the securing of financial support. It is appreciated that much of this information is already available elsewhere. The intention here is simply to provide an overview of some of the available options which are of specific relevance to nurses and therapies staff. It is an appropriate beginning for a book intended to assist the potential PhD student and has stimulated me to refocus my thoughts on the issue and access some money!

NURSES AND PhD STUDIES

An increasing number of nurses are undertaking PhDs, a trend to be welcomed, despite its detractors. Financing PhD studies has often been a tricky issue for students inside and out of nursing. The pattern for many in disciplines other than nursing seems to be attendance at university in order to undertake a first degree and then either career entry or, for some, a prolongation of university studies in order to complete an MPhil/PhD. The years on a student's income may be hard and quite long but they are often over in early adulthood and herald the start of what may well be lucrative employment. Whilst conceivably this education pathway may come to be the pattern for nursing (although, sadly, not the lucrative career) it is not generally the case at the time of writing. Instead, nurses wishing to undertake PhD studies have often been qualified for several years and have reached a position both professionally and personally that precludes a return to a student income. Indeed, Traynor and Rafferty (1998) identified that the majority of PhD studies undertaken by nurses between 1976 and 1993 acknowledged no funding source. The implication is that despite the prolonged cries for academic advancement and research in nursing, most (nursing) PhD students have been self-funding.

However, the political and professional landscape has changed since 1993 and there appears to be an increasing appreciation (desperation?), for a variety of reasons, of the need to 'grow' more nurses educated to doctoral level and beyond. The move of nursing education into higher education has necessitated the re-thinking of nursing in relation to research. Contemporary concerns include: the need to build the research capacity; promoting awareness of the important political aspects of research; and the need for improved access to research funding (Traynor and Rafferty, 1998). What this means is that many staff in university departments and in trusts see the need for a cadre of nurses who can undertake research, contribute to both practice and professional development from a research perspective, teach on research, supervise research, publish research and bring in research-related monies. Staff who meet these criteria are valuable commodities. Against this backdrop, the case for funding nurses on PhD programmes may well be reviewed favourably by (enlightened) management.

Study options appear to be as follows: PhDs may be undertaken on a part-time or a full-time basis. Students undertaking part-time PhDs are normally required to submit their thesis within a time frame of between four and six years from the point of registration. However, colleagues tell me of increasing pressure from some funding bodies to complete part-time doctorates within four years whilst other universities have extended the part-time allowance to as much as eight years. Advantages of undertaking a PhD part-time seem to include having more than three years to immerse oneself in a variety of literature, to develop and refine one's ideas and to enjoy the mental space afforded by a less pressurised timetable. Moreover, current earnings continue (and may even rise) whilst also being a student of sorts. The disadvantages lie in the length of time available in which to become unfocused, demotivated and exhausted by the research endeavour (conducted after work and often in unsociable hours). It is difficult to pursue and consolidate ideas whilst also trying to undertake a full time job and the 'shelf-life' of the original ideas may be limited. There is a constant struggle to find sufficient space to achieve a reasonable 'chunk' of work. Family and social life may also pay a heavy price. Indeed, life events (births, marriages, deaths and so on) have a greater probability of occurence over a six-year rather than a three-year period. 'Time out' for data collection and writing up is advisable and needs to be negotiated at an early stage, not least regarding the details of financial arrangements during this time. Thus, the general consensus of opinion suggests that full-time study is hard but ultimately more preferable to the part-time variety.

Yet, for many, as already indicated, this is not an option. For those of us undertaking part-time study the funding arrangements frequently involve a 'trade-off' between time (study leave) and contribution to university fees. It is very rare to get 100% of the fees paid and luxurious amounts of time away from the workplace while still receiving a full salary. That having been said, at least one university nursing department has adopted a policy of 'fast tracking' staff through PhDs. The price to be paid for having both PhD time and money appears to be reduced control over the focus of the inquiry (having to research someone else's ideas/agenda), pressure to complete within the allotted time and reliance on colleagues to 'pick-up' the workload abandoned in favour of the PhD study. Moreover, some university nursing departments, particularly in the light of the Research Assessment Exercise (RAE) where every PhD student counts, are requiring their staff to undertake PhDs within their own university. This is irrespective of whether this fits the PhD student's academic bill. Clearly these are all issues that require consideration at the outset of any intended study.

All sources of funding will require information from the applicant on what (and whom) it is they want to study, why, where and with what potential benefits. A vague sentence about contributing to the body of knowledge is unlikely to be sufficient. An indication of how the project is to be managed in terms of feasibility, time frame, and anticipated costs is usually required and, increasingly, applicants are asked to comment on their career intentions. Any sources of funding already secured must be made transparent and usually a comment is required on why these are considered inadequate. In addition many funding sources (such as regional awards and the Medical Research Council) require a research proposal to scrutinise, often with ethical approval for the study having already been obtained. Naturally, when applying to particular bodies for funding, the area of inquiry should correspond with the interests of the (potential) supporting body. An important point to convey (and certainly my own experience) is that many sources of PhD funding for nurses appear to favour assisting those who are not already employed by a higher education institution. It would appear that if you are a university lecturer it is assumed, perhaps expected, that the employing university will facilitate the professional/research development of its own staff.

An additional point is the need to communicate the intention to apply for funding to other relevant personnel, particularly project supervisors and current employers. Funding agencies require details on the university in which the PhD is to be registered and the names of the intended supervisors, so these have to be thought through in advance of application. If an application for financial help involving secondment from the workplace is being made, then a supporting statement from the employer is requested as well as details of current salary. The names of independent, professional and academic referees may also be sought. Each of these 'stakeholders' is likely to have to complete a different section of the application form within a certain time frame. Planning well in advance for this is vital if the application is to be submitted in time and have the optimum chance of success. Funders often require up to 12 copies of the application form which have to be provided by the applicant. Sometimes application forms are available in disk format which facilitates their completion. Usually, details on form completion are very specific, for example script size, line spacing and so on, and these points must be observed. As many funding sources make clear, late, incomplete and faxed applications will not be considered. It is also worth noting that most funding sources will require an annual report, and continuation of financial support will often depend on satisfactory progress. Unsuccessful applicants to funding bodies are usually permitted to reapply after a specified time frame. It is worth checking the small print. Feedback on the quality of applications for unsuccessful (and often successful) applicants is usually not forthcoming due to the increase in workload this would represent.

FUNDING SOURCES

Perhaps the most useful information source regarding funding for PhDs is the new database of R&D funding opportunities currently available on the Internet. It is called RD Info: A Digest of Health Related Research Funding and Training Opportunities, and can be found at: http://www.leeds.ac.uk/rdinfo/. It is an excellent resource and lists funding sources, types of grants available and the amount of money provided. Details on submission deadlines are also available as well as comprehensive information regarding the research interests of the funder. It is beyond the remit of this chapter to duplicate all the information available on this website. The purpose of the following section is simply to make a few general points regarding application for funding and highlight some of the options available.

FUNDING FROM EMPLOYER

This is the most obvious place to start and has been previously referred to mainly in relation to university staff (nursing) who wish to undertake PhDs. Each university has its own policy on staff development/study leave and scholarly activity. Obviously potential PhD students need to make themselves aware of this. It is also clear that some trusts have started funding a few of their clinical staff to undertake PhDs. Again this is usually on a part-time basis and the numbers are currently very low.

One trust with which I am familiar is meeting the university fees for one of their staff to undertake a PhD. Time in which to conduct the study has yet to be organised and any additional expenses, such as travel to an alternative site, are not being met. Funding for these is having to be sought elsewhere. Another London trust with an excellent research reputation and, crucially, a nursing director who firmly believes in the importance of nursing research has organised full-time opportunities for staff to study to PhD level. She has formed a partnership with a university department with which the trust shares a common research interest. Together the university and trust have applied successfully for research monies from the Economic and Social Research Council (ESRC) for specific projects. Advertisements are placed in the professional press inviting nurses to apply to undertake the project, which then acts as a vehicle for them to obtain a PhD. The trust provides the field site for the research (acting essentially as an 'industrial placement') while the university offers full-time supervision. Whilst the funding body provides a stipend for the student of approximately £10,000 per annum, the trust is required to provide an additional contribution of at least £2,000 per annum and meet travel costs of the researcher, and to contribute to university fees. There are also 'hidden' costs of time, accommodation and so on. Thus, for a three-year period the trust has to provide at least £10,000 per student which, in the case in question, was bid for within the trust on the basis of developing the R&D capacity. In return the PhD students are required to raise the profile of nursing research within the the trust in a number of ways and demonstrate their progress via relevant publications throughout the course of undertaking their study. The lessons to be learnt from this example concern the value of a research-aware manager and the skills demonstrated in capitalising on a climate receptive to developing the R&D 'workforce'.

Research 'training and development' awards from region

Research Awards within the gift of NHSE Regional administration appear to have replaced awards previously overseen by the Department of Health Research and Development division. In most regions these are annual awards managed by the Education and Training Sub-Group of the R&D department. Work is currently in progress to ensure that administration and organisation of these awards is harmonised across different NHS regions. Essentially, applicants, working in practice, bid for financial support for a three-year period of study at an approved university which will result in a PhD. Awards are generally held at universities within the region's boundary and are open to nurses and the professions allied to medicine as well as to doctors. Applications in line with the ambitions of the NHS R&D initiative are welcome particularly from those with a background in primary care and/or an interest in decision analysis, service delivery and organisational issues. Competition for such support is notoriously very difficult and awards are made on the quality of the submitted proposal, the supervision offered, the research-training capabilities of the host institution and the considered potential of the applicant for a career in health services research. Support and advice on strengthening research proposals for submission is offered. The application form has four components: applicant's form, supervisor's form, Fellowship agreement form (to be completed by the administrative officer in the academic institution where the research will be based) and referee's form. Successful applicants become employees of the host institution. The NHSE allocates a predetermined sum of money for each Fellowship to the host institution for a period of 36 months. They also contribute £4,500 to the host institution to cover such items as travelling expenses, research materials and office consumables. The awards are usually advertised in *The Guardian*, the *Health Services Journal* and the *Nursing Times* and contain details of the submission deadline. Results of applications are conveyed by July in order that the successful candidate may commence studies in the following academic year. Details of the funding opportunities in Scotland may be found on the Nursing Research Initiative for Scotland website at: http://fhis.gcal.ac.uk/nris/opening.html.

AWARDS FROM THE RESEARCH COUNCILS

There are seven research councils in the UK which provide support for postgraduate studentships. (Support for postgraduate studies in Northern Ireland is provided by the Department of Education Northern Ireland.) The two councils of particular interest to nurses and therapists are the Economic and Social Research Council (ESRC) and the Medical Research Council (MRC). As their names imply, their research interests are different but both offer a variety of award schemes and the details on these can best be accessed by contacting them directly (see below) and via their joint home page on the Internet, http://www.nerc.ac.uk/research-councils/. ESRC details are on http://www.esrc.ac.uk/grants.html with specific details for post-graduates on http://www.esrc.ac.uk/postgrad.html. Those relating to the MRC can be found by using their search facility and typing in Research Grants http://www.mrc.ac.uk.

The MRC (20 Park Crescent, London W1N 4AL) provides research training schemes for all stages of a non-clinical and clinical research career. Details of the MRC's various personal award schemes are normally advertised in publications such as *Nature, British Medical Journal* and *The Lancet*. The scheme of relevance to nursing staff is the Clinical Training Fellowship, the intended outcome of which is a PhD. The tenure of this award is three years although part-time awards are available. Applicants for this scheme are considered twice a year, in February and September. Applicants from a nursing, midwifery or therapies background are particularly welcomed and two fellowships are earmarked specifically for these individuals. Short-listed candidates are interviewed in February (following a September application) and July. Decisions regarding applications are communicated within five months of the closing date of the scheme. Nurse applicants and members of the Professions Allied to Medicine should have completed their professional training and hold a Masters or equivalent postgraduate research-orientated qualification. The application form is in four parts, each of which require completion by a variety of people, such as the applicant, head of department, proposed supervisor and independent referee and it is the responsibility of the applicant to co-ordinate the submission. As with Fellowships supported by region, the quality of the proposal is judged alongside the potential of the host institution to provide a high quality/appropriate research training environment. Applicants are encouraged to broaden their experience by moving away from departments in which they are currently working and the chosen institution will have to provide comment on the structure of the research support offered over the three years of the award. Clearly this is intended to reduce the amount of PhD students 'left to their own devices', unsupported through the time of their studies. Again, the format is that the MRC reimburses the salary of the Clinical Training Fellow who, for the duration of the Fellowship, becomes an employee of the host institution, that is the university in which the PhD is to be registered. The MRC also makes financial support available to the host institution in recognition of the research training provided and a travel allowance is made available to the student. Telephone and e-mail enquiries regarding these awards can be directed to the Research Career Awards (Fellowships) Section at MRC head office (0171-636 5422, e-mail: fellows@headoffice.mrc.ac.uk).

The ESRC Studentships (Polaris House, North Star Avenue, Swindon SN2 1UJ) may be held on a full-time or part-time basis at a number of ESRC recognised higher education departments with provision in the Social Sciences (see below). These departments often advertise the post-graduate studentships they have available in the research section of *The Guardian* (currently published on Tuesdays). Graduates from any discipline may apply for ESRC funding as long as they meet certain academic and residential requirements. Again, there is considerable emphasis on meeting the research training components of a PhD. Institutions recognised by the ESRC are classified as either Mode A or Mode B (or both A and B). Mode A means that adequate research training is provided for the student in the first year of their research programme. Applicants should only apply to a Mode B department if they have already received a foundation in research training. ESRC part-time studentships are not available to those employed in diploma and/or degree awarding institutions or if the employer has funded employees to undertake doctoral level studies in the social sciences within the last five years. Deadline for submission is usually early May and candidates are informed of the results before the end of July. Enquiries regarding these awards and details of the ESRC departments approved for the receipt of ESRC studentships can be directed to the Postgraduate Training Division, 01793 413043, e-mail: ptd@esrc.ac.uk. The guidance notes for applicants are particularly helpful.

RESEARCH GRANTS FROM STATUTORY BODIES (NATIONAL BOARDS, UKCC, RCN AND RCM)

Details of research bursaries available from the national boards need to be requested on an individual basis. The United Kingdom Central Council (UKCC) established an annual research scholarship award in 1998 for projects of relevance to the work of the UKCC. It is worth £20,000 per year for two years but might be a useful platform from which to commence PhD level study. Research awards are offered on a competitive basis and details of how to apply are published in their newsletter *Register*. In addition the Royal College of Nursing (RCN) has an awards scheme open to RCN members. Details of available scholarships may be requested from the awards office. The Royal College of Midwives (RCM) also has monies available for the educational/ research development of its members (see Jacob and Wason, 1998). The college has a relationship with a number of sponsors and funding opportunities arise on a regular basis. Details of these are advertised in relevant professional journals.

RESEARCH MONIES FROM CHARITABLE ORGANISATIONS, FOUNDATIONS AND OTHER SOURCES

There are a number of charities which offer research monies to nurses on a competition-prize basis or in the form of grants. The Fellowships are generally intended to fund research in the area of particular interest to the charity and lead to improved quality of patient care. The Association of Medical Charities Handbook (free on 0171 404 6454) identifies many of these as does The Grants Register 1995-1997 published by Macmillan (Curzio, 1998). Those charities identified below are but a fraction of those who support research fellowships within their specific field; it may be worth looking at a current voluntary sector/health care directory (Vousden, 1999) for other possible sources.

The Cancer Research Campaign (CRC) offers a CRC nursing research fellowship on an annual basis, in educational/psychosocial aspects of cancer. The award is designed to lead to the presentation of a PhD. The Fellowship is said to provide an appropriate salary in line with the applicant's current salary plus research running expenses and fees. Further information about the CRC's education and psychosocial research activities can be found on the CRC website: www.crc.org.uk and details of the awards can be obtained from the Director of Education Programmes (0171 317 5188). AVERT, the Aids Virus Education and Research Trust, also awards postgraduate studentship with annual grants of £7,500 for three years, again designed to lead to the presentation of a PhD. The National Eczema Society fund PhD research studentships, as does The British Heart Foundation (BHF). The awards are normally for current salary. Details on the BHF scheme may be obtained by contacting the Research Funds Manager (0171 935 0185).

Another well established supporter of nursing research is the Smith and Nephew Foundation (Smith and Nephew Foundation, 2 Temple Place, London WC2R 3BP). The Foundation offers two types of research awards to nurses and midwives. Scholarships are offered for those wishing to undertake Masters level studies. Fellowships are awarded to experienced nurses undertaking PhD projects. They are designed to allow individuals to be seconded from their posts in order to undertake data collection or analysis. The value of the awards is up to £30,000 for one year. Applicants are required, as in most cases, to complete an application form and submit a research proposal. Written confirmation of support is also required from the project supervisor and the employer. Details of the award scheme are advertised in the professional press or may be obtained by contacting the Foundation Administrator (0171 836 7922).

It is always worth scouring the professional press and the research opportunities pages of *The Guardian* for details of research grants available. *Nursing Times* also runs a research section in its appointments pages wherein research training opportunities are published regularly. Details of the Sir Kenneth Calman Bursaries and the Robert Baxter Fellowship schemes have recently been advertised. These are supported by the High Security Psychiatric Services Commissioning Board R&D Committee and include PhD programmes. Applications are particularly welcome from nurses, social workers and other professions allied to medicine.

CONCLUDING THOUGHTS

The intention of this chapter has been to bring together information from a variety of sources regarding potential avenues to be explored for PhD funding. Whilst finding funds to enable one to undertake PhD studies is important, virtually all the PhD students I spoke to considered funding to be a relatively straightforward issue in comparison to other hurdles which they are finding themselves having to negotiate. One student, a regional award winner, talked of the 'culture shock' she experienced on entering the academic department in which she is currently located. She described the goals and philosophy of the department to be radically different to those with which she was familiar in the NHS. She also talked of the newness of nurses in some academic departments and their perceived need to prove their worth. For her, the transition from senior NHS employee to PhD student, with resultant change of identity, was at times a disturbing experience and the need for support networks was very important. Moreover, although grateful for her research opportunity, the three-year funding does not equate with her previous salary and she has had to make significant life-style changes as a result, and budgeting has required her to ascertain precisely when the funding is to be stopped.

Another colleague who was funded by a charitable organisation to conduct a part-time PhD talked of the ease with which the funding was obtained but the lack of time available in which to conduct the study. (The charity had met her university expenses for the duration of the registration although she remained in full-time employment.) This colleague also highlighted the important and sensitive nature of PhD supervision. A doctor with whom she was working and a nurse academic (at the university in which she was registered) supervised her. Whilst the multidisciplinary approach was enriching it also presented a difficult dynamic over the exact focus of the study. Predictably, perhaps, the nursing and the medical viewpoints were not always convergent. Moreover when she changed her employment the supervision from the medical practitioner was no longer forthcoming. The lessons she learnt from the experience were the need to consider very carefully the choice of supervisor, the stability of supervisor and self in current employment and the thorny issue of who has a legitimate 'say' in the direction of the PhD. Her advice for potential PhD students is to only research something of interest to yourself and think carefully about the choice of external examiner. Rather like funding, this is a practical, academic and political issue.

For me, the problems lie in negotiating work commitments, research time and caring for a young family. However, although the situation is difficult, it is not, as yet, impossible. Interestingly, I have a work colleague who is approaching his PhD from a sociological viewpoint. He has no taught component to his degree and is particularly familiar with the literature in his field since he has been teaching sociology (to nurses) for many years. Consequently he does not not feel he is 'starting from scratch'. Yet if the enquiry is to be located in a relevant but less familiar discipline (in my case, medical anthropology), the taught component, associated assignments and 'new' literature present additional challenges on the PhD path. Whilst engaging with medical anthropology has been (and is) an intellectual joy/revelation to me, this 'new kid on the block' academic experience and its implications for achieving high academic goals is something I had not fully appreciated at the study outset. It makes funding issues seem easy.

REFERENCES

Curzio, J. (1998) Funding for evidence-based nursing practice in the UK. *Nursing Times Research*; 3: 2, 100–107.

Jacob, S., Wason, P. (1998) The process of applying for funding. (Scholarships to assist midwives with their professional development.) *Midwives' Journal* (RCM). May; 1: 5, 156–157.

McMahon, A. (1997) Implications for nursing of the NHS R&D funding policy. *Nursing Standard*; 11: 28, 32–33.

Tarling, M., Crofts, L. (1998) *The Essential Researcher's Handbook for Nurses and Health Care Professionals.* London: Baillière Tindall.

Traynor, M., Rafferty, A.M. (1998) *Nursing Research and the Higher Education Context: A Second Working Paper.* London: Centre for Policy in Nursing Research.

Vousden, M. (1999) *The Nursing Times Directory of Health Care Information and Resources.* London: NT Books.

FURTHER READING

Baker, M., Kirk, S. (1996) *Research and Development for the NHS: Evidence, Evaluation and Effectiveness.* Oxford: Radcliffe Medical Press.

Castledine, G. (1994) Finding funds for nursing research. *British Journal of Nursing*; 3: 22, 1197.

Moorbath, P. (1992) Availability of grants for nursing research. *Nursing Standard*; 6: 29, 25–27.

Traynor, M., Rafferty, A.M. (1997) *The NHS R&D Context for Nursing Research*. London: Centre for Policy in Nursing Research.

NHS R&D FUNDING

Task Force on R&D in the NHS (1994) *Supporting Research and Development in the NHS* (Culyer report). London: HMSO.

Department of Health (NHSME) (1997) *Strategic Framework for the Use of the NHS RD Levy*. London: HMSO.

Department of Health (NHSME) (1997) *R&D Support Funding for NHS Providers: An Introduction*. London: HMSO.

Department of Health (NHSME) (1997) *Department of Health and NHS Funding for Research and Development*. London: HMSO.

Department of Health (NHSME) (1997) *R&D Support Funding for NHS Providers from 1998/99*. London: HMSO.

These documents may be obtained by writing to: Health Publications Unit, PO Box 410, Wetherby, Yorkshire LS2 3LN.

3. Ethical considerations in undertaking higher degree research

Author
Trudy Stevens

Commentary
Professor Judith Lathlean

INTRODUCTION

This chapter focuses on the ethical considerations within higher degree research, highlighting those relating to the process, the methodology and the topic being studied. These aspects are illustrated through discussion of an ethnographic study that was undertaken as part of an extensive evaluation of a project implementing a radical change in the delivery of maternity care within one NHS trust. Trudy Stevens was initially employed as a research assistant to undertake the ethnography. It later became the subject of her PhD with Judith Lathlean as her co-supervisor.

The chapter has, in the main, been written by Trudy Stevens and she describes her experience in the first person. Judith Lathlean provides the commentary at the end and highlights some of the key issues.

ONE-TO-ONE MIDWIFERY PRACTICE

In 1993 an innovative new style of midwifery practice was introduced into a city-based maternity service. Fulfilling the recommendations made in the Expert Maternity Group's report, *Changing Childbirth* (DoH, 1993), this was the first team to have implemented what subsequently became government policy for the maternity services. Supporting the tenets of choice, control and continuity of carer for women during pregnancy and childbirth, this project offered greater autonomy and responsibility to midwives, counterbalancing the previously dominant position of obstetricians. The change was radical and the potential for interprofessional tensions disrupting both the project and conventional service delivery was very real.

In view of the pilot nature of the project, a multidimensional evaluation was designed as integral to its implementation. Using a comparative control design, four aspects were considered: user responses to the service; clinical audit of standards and adherence to targets; an economic evaluation; and a study of the change process and its impact on professionals delivering care. (The first two years of the main study have been reported by McCourt and Page, 1996.)

As a midwife and social scientist, I was appointed to undertake the fourth arm of the evaluation – the exploration of its impact on professionals. The research approach was described in the evaluation protocol as an 'ethnographic case study'. Ethnography seeks to understand a social situation from the perspectives of those involved in it. Frequently it entails the researcher being in the field for an extended period, collecting data using a variety of techniques in order to achieve an in-depth understanding of the setting. I was involved in the study for more than four years, using interviews, observation and documentary analyses as the data collection techniques. However, less formal methods also proved important in enriching understanding and sensitising me to issues that needed to be explored more formally.

This methodology has the advantage of uncovering the views of both the powerful and the less obvious groups involved, determining whether particular issues hold different significance for different people. Thus I collected data from obstetricians and midwives at all levels of experience, as well as the managers involved in the service development.

By exploring staff reactions to the implementation and development of this radical change, enabling the voices of both those involved and those peripheral to the project to be heard, this study provided a strong ethical dimension to the service development. Nevertheless, the process by which the work was achieved involved many other ethical considerations, some obvious and inherent in all research, others less expected and becoming apparent as the work progressed.

SETTING UP THE ETHNOGRAPHIC STUDY

Initially, there are concerns to do with the use of limited resources and the value of the research. Funding is generally scarce and the time of participants, researcher and supervisors is equally precious. Inappropriate, thus unethical, use of these resources can be avoided at the planning stage by the development of a detailed research proposal guided by experienced researchers. Areas that need to be considered include ensuring that the research question is useful and needs to be addressed, that it is focused enough to enable the researcher to obtain suitable data, and that the methodology chosen will generate such data. The researcher needs to have the skills, knowledge and resources to undertaken the work. Other considerations include the suitability of the study site and participants in terms of numbers and accessibility, and that concurrent research or issues of control and hierarchy will not unduly influence the findings.

Originally, the wider evaluation protocol for the project had undergone extensive development with the assistance of a group of nationally recognised researchers, though the details of the ethnographic study needed to be formulated. The importance of the research area to be addressed was clear, and the methodology selected appeared highly appropriate. Although a relative novice at research, my previous overseas work and academic studies had convinced me of the value of the anthropological perspective, and I was developing my knowledge through an MSc in research methods. My access to the site was apparently welcomed and the study facilitated in the most positive way. Ethically everything appeared in place. However, two issues arose which were later to have an important influence on my work.

The first difficulty lay in trying to formulate clear and defined research questions that met the needs of a research protocol. My remit had been broad and obvious – to monitor the change process and explore the implications for professionals – whereas breaking this down into distinct questions was less clear. For quantitative studies, particularly those which seek to prove a cause and effect relationship, the task is relatively straightforward; the situation is slightly more difficult in ethnographic studies which seek participants' understandings of a situation. Fearful of imposing a particular frame, one seeks to be open and responsive to the perspectives of the people being studied. Thus the questions I formulated were not tightly defined but took the form of issues to be focused on:

► What is the effect of caseload practice on the midwives working this way?

► How has the project implementation affected the structure and culture of the hospital?

► How was the change process negotiated by the staff involved?

Throughout the data collection period I found there was a constant tension between being open and responsive to new ideas whilst remaining focused enough on particular issues to gain sufficient data to be able to draw robust conclusions, without defining the boundaries and becoming blinkered to other possibly more important consequences. Inevitably I ended up with an enormous amount of data, some of which may never be used. Although the result of an ethical approach, this situation is perhaps itself unethical.

This more open and receptive approach had other consequences. Several of the senior obstetricians, whom I viewed as important 'gatekeepers', were experienced researchers in the clinical field. Occasionally, during the negotiating stage prior to commencement of an interview, I felt as if I was being 'grilled' as my methodology was scrutinised. Although supportive of the work I was undertaking, their expertise lay in different paradigms and their advice was framed accordingly. For example, I was strongly advised to 'define my hypothesis more clearly' and later on an obstetric research fellow's response to a presentation I gave was 'interesting but anecdotal'. Undoubtedly the valuation placed on my work by the obstetricians would have been higher had I heeded the advice presented and altered my methodology and questions, but this clearly was not appropriate. Fortunately, this valuation did not appear to unduly affect their response once I had engaged them during interview.

A more fundamental consequence of adopting this research approach related to funding when the hoped-for regional support was not forthcoming. This second complication held important implications for the ethnographic study. Initially I found that time which could have been used for data collection was needed for the submission of various funding proposals, a frustrating situation compounded by rejections which were based on nervousness about the methodology to be employed. Difficulty in obtaining funding for qualitative studies within the health service is well recognised (Lathlean, 1996a), and may, as in this instance, highlight the gap between the perspectives of the funding bodies and health service managers who were demanding answers to questions this work would address. Eventually my study was undertaken with the support of a Smith and Nephew Nursing Research Fellowship award and then by the development of a researcher-practitioner post in which I undertook clinical duties and some teaching as well as the research. Although unplanned, this situation presented some advantages including a longer exposure to, and personal experiences of, the study area – phenomena supported within ethnographic research.

On the down side, because information from this study was in demand nationally as other projects were developed along similar lines, I felt a moral and real imperative to publish as quickly as possible. Nevertheless, publications based on interim analyses might prove unsubstantiated by subsequent work and this could jeopardise the whole study. Moreover, it would be unethical to present definitive findings until they could be fully substantiated. The partial solution to this was to present conference papers which enabled the work to be made public and discussed in a less formal manner than through publication.

ETHICS COMMITTEE APPROVAL

Research Ethics Committees (RECs) undertake an independent ethical review of research proposals in order to safeguard the interests of participants in respect of inappropriate designs and the avoidance of potential harm. Such scrutiny is generally part of the 'gatekeeping' process required by most organisations prior to granting access for research; frequently major funding bodies require proof of REC approval to be submitted with funding applications, and many universities have RECs to scrutinise research undertaken by their academics or students. Formal approval from an REC is required for any work undertaken on National Health Service clients, client records, staff or facilities.

However, as highlighted by Tierney (1995), in her study of RECs within the Scottish Health Service, the composition and efficiency of these committees may vary, and adherence to their requirements may not be checked. Frequently their membership is dominated by doctors whose expertise lies within quantitative research; both review protocols and the review process have a medical rather than sociological research orientation. Unfamiliarity with different research approaches can result in protocols being unjustifiably refused, or may be approved when tighter controls are applied. Overwhelmed by the number of applications, some local RECs are reported to take up to two years for approval to be granted (Pickering, 1996). In order to avoid this lengthy process, many small-scale studies may circumnavigate REC scrutiny under the guise of quality assessment or audit exercises. As Pickering (1996) suggests, the appropriate composition and education of RECs constitutes an important ethical dimension.

In the movement towards the establishment of more varied RECs, with the strengthening of consumer and nursing perspectives, health services researchers may be confused as to where they should submit their proposal: university, NHS or trust. Each group may offer a different, potentially conflicting, perspective. For example, tension may arise between NHS RECs which act as an impartial reviewing body for research undertaken within the health service and trust RECs who wish to retain control of work undertaken on their premises. The potential for biased reviews cannot be ignored from trusts wishing to establish or maintain a particular research profile. However, local control can be helpful in protecting participants from being over-researched, a situation highlighted by Buckingham (1996) whose study on a children's ward coincided with two other projects conducted by medical students.

My own contact with the local REC demonstrates an interesting perspective on how the situation is changing. In line with the requirement that any research undertaken within the NHS requires approval from the local REC, formal approval was sought and given for the large scale evaluation of which this study was a part. Once it was determined that the duration of this study would exceed the initial evaluative work, I sought confirmation of approval for its continuation separate from the wider evaluation. However, at this time approval was deemed unnecessary as I was not approaching clients.

The opportunity for exploitation of any participant is present in all research and relates just as much to the professionals offering care as those receiving it. At that time the committee obviously held the belief that the staff would be able to refuse to participate without consequence. This is questionable. Certainly the midwives recruited to the project acknowledged their integral involvement in the research and, in the main, obstetricians are confident enough to refuse to participate in midwifery-related studies. However, the reality of more junior staff being viewed as a 'captive audience', being reluctant to refuse for fear of stigma or repercussions on their career, should not be overlooked.

The potential vulnerability of health care students is now recognised and their university's REC approval may be required if students are approached. However, my work commenced before the movement to university status and at that time formal approval to recruit midwifery students was not an issue. Nevertheless, members of the midwifery school were closely involved in the project implementation and evaluation and were fully aware of any student involvement. Official permission was not sought from the midwifery school but from individual students in a manner that enabled their refusal to participate without fear of any consequence.

RESEARCHER-PRACTITIONERS AND FIELD ROLES

Some unique ethical dilemmas are presented to researchers who are also practitioners in the area studied. These relate to their approach to the work, issues of deception in field roles adopted and personal-professional responsibilities.

The practice of research being undertaken by members of the 'community' studied is not new. When research is undertaken by someone who is familiar with the setting, it can be argued that their tacit knowledge (Polanyi, 1967) of that community is an invaluable aid in controlling their effect on the study situation and in facilitating effective communication with the study participants.

However, such approaches have been viewed with scepticism, being thought to entail an inherent subjectivity with the researcher-practitioner unable to theoretically disentangle themselves from their work. The difficulty in maintaining research awareness within a familiar setting, not inadvertently imposing your own 'world view' on the setting, has to be recognised. Hammersley (1992) warned that self-knowledge is not immediately given; people can deceive themselves and may have an interest in self-deception. As Reed and Proctor (1995) highlighted, practitioners have both a history and a future in their profession. Their knowledge about the wider context of the study may be extremely detailed but they will invariably carry value judgements and expectations concerning practice and the development of the profession. Such values need to be acknowledged and accounted for when undertaking practitioner research. Thus close liaison with an academic department, exposing the work to the rigorous scrutiny of a research community, is particularly desirable.

Despite the difficulties, practitioner research offers valuable perspectives, particularly in health care. Lipson (1991) comments that, although the goals of nursing and research are different, the skills and qualities that enhance rapport and trust are similar. She re-emphasises that the best data grows out of relationships in which the informants trust the researcher, and the researcher has a grasp of their own influence on the interaction. However, an ethical dilemma may arise as the researcher defines the role that they will assume within the study setting (field role). Participants may alter their behaviour in the presence of experienced practitioners, so biasing important data, but deception offers little to the development of relationships based on trust.

Covert research is now rarely considered appropriate, except perhaps for studies of deviant communities. Nevertheless, it is not uncommon for researcher-practitioners to be economical with the truth about the extent of their clinical experience or to emphasise some aspects rather than others. For example, Ersser (1996) described how he was known as a research nurse but that his youthful appearance helped him avoid disclosure of his tutor status. Like him, I found that, in my 'impression management' (Goffman, 1959) of a situation, I would stress particular aspects of my 'biography' according to the participants. Apparently nurses viewed Ersser as 'a researcher who was also a nurse' while to patients he was 'a nurse doing some research'; to obstetricians I attempted to portray the academically credible social scientist, engaged in PhD studies, who also happened to be a midwife, but to midwives I created a more empathetic environment by stressing my midwifery orientation.

The work may also carry personal difficulties for the practitioner researcher. In his ethnographic study of the police, Young (1991) highlighted how a new awareness of what was previously accepted may appear ludicrous or morally indefensible. Furthermore, what does the practitioner-researcher do if they witness 'bad practice'? To which code of ethics do they adhere – the research community's or the profession's? These may conflict, particularly over issues of confidentiality. The problems of revelation and betrayal are a part of all qualitative research but are particularly acute if the researcher wishes to continue to practice in their profession.

A more frequent decision may arise when the researcher is placed in a situation which demands their clinical skills in the course of their research activities. The dilemma of whether to act as nurse or researcher can be difficult to resolve and may change as the study progresses. In his study, Ersser considered it inappropriate to assist a patient-participant as a nurse and so called for assistance, whereas Buckingham decided that her primary concern for the child dictated that she would intervene to assist a child in pain if required (Ersser, 1996; Buckingham, 1996). As observation within the clinical setting did not form a major component of my work I was rarely faced with this dilemma. However, I decided that client care superseded other considerations and, should the need arise, I would intervene – but only when essential, and then in a manner that was likely to have least effect on my relationships with the midwives and the research.

Role confusion is a potential problem, though in the clinical field I found people occasionally mixed my roles on purpose. For example, one sister called me saying, 'I know you are not here doing your research, but come here and look at this, I want you to see,' showing me a delivery room recently vacated by a project midwife but left in a particularly dirty condition with resuscitation equipment left uncleaned. However, as time progressed people forgot my research role as I became a familiar, available and trusted colleague. Although this was highly desirable in terms of minimising my impact on the study setting, I wondered if this was moving into the realms of covert work. Was it ethical to use information gained in this manner? For example, having discussed some difficulties with project personnel, one manager exclaimed: 'You are not going to use that in your research, are you?' As I considered I had no purpose to be on site apart from for the research, this questioned my presence and highlighted the need to frequently restate my research role.

The tension between being so relaxed and enabling people to confide as a friend rather than a researcher yet conducting ethical research was clearly apparent. In recognition that such familiarity could generate some degree of role confusion, I considered it unethical to use data collected when individuals were apparently confiding in me as a colleague they felt they could trust and unburden upon. However, following particularly insightful discussions I might ask if I could use some of the points in my research, a request that was commonly granted. If this appeared inappropriate or permission was refused I could not 'forget' what I had learnt but made a mental note to explore the issue in future data collection episodes without recording the exact nature of the incident under discussion. Thus such conversations sensitised me to something which could later be explored in a theoretical rather than factual sense.

CONSENT

Research requires that 'informed consent' be freely obtained from all participants prior to their involvement, and that having freely joined the study they may withdraw at any subsequent stage without repercussion. However, the nature of informed consent is not without problems. Homan (1991) offered the following definition:

Informed =

(a) that all pertinent aspects of what is to occur and what might occur are disclosed to the subject;

(b) that the subject should be able to comprehend this information.

Consent =

(c) that the subject is competent to make a rational and mature judgement;

(d) that the agreement to participate should be voluntary, free from coercion and undue influence.

In qualitative studies, consent may not necessarily be clearly defined as a one-off event, there being many layers to each situation:

▶ *Consent to be approached, particularly in the work situation.* Formal permission may be required from authority figures to approach individuals, for example manager or ward sister, then from individuals personally. This may be undertaken in the form of a letter rather than an initial personal contact.

▶ *Consent to participate in the study.* This involves providing explanations about the study and negotiating data collection arrangements, that is the accepted 'informed consent' procedure. However, the amount of information provided may be influenced by communication difficulties, translation barriers and by the participant's wishes; many may seek very full explanations but others may choose not to know and express uninterest while readily agreeing to participate. I was surprised at how many of my participants, including senior doctors, appeared quite uninterested in the information I offered, frequently cutting off my explanations.

▶ *Level of participation.* Less information is likely to be given to participants who are thought to be peripheral to the study; however, if, as the study develops, these become key informants, the consent issue may need to be renegotiated. Also, obtaining the consent of everyone involved in observational studies is difficult – the major actors, for example doctors and midwives, are obvious but there are others such as cleaners or families who are peripheral to the focus.

▶ *Degree of participation.* Although agreeing to participate the respondent may choose to be guarded or unreserved and frank, or indeed even control the data collection for their personal agenda. Although this constitutes an informal form of consent, how justified is the researcher to 'force', by whatever skilful means, the participant to respond in the way desired?

In my study, although consent to undertake the work had been given at the outset, I considered it not only polite but also prudent to keep the clinical director and midwifery managers informed of my progress and my proposed plans. Perhaps by taking the initiative I pre-empted any interference, but certainly no concern was ever demonstrated in my presence and I found my access to all categories of staff was well facilitated. For example, unit sisters helped to organise focus group interviews with staff, while medical secretaries assisted my meetings with consultant obstetricians, one even phoning me on the off-chance saying, 'Quick, catch him now, he's free and in a good mood!' This assistance clearly had an ethical dimension as it was particularly important in ensuring my work did not interfere with general care provision.

Prior to undertaking any formal data collection work, I sent the proposed participants a letter outlining the study, my reason for approaching them and my proposed method of data collection. At the start of each data collection procedure I reiterated these points and confirmed their understanding of the work, negotiating an agreement before commencing.

For the project midwives' participation in the research evaluation was part of their job description and a member of the research team was involved in the interviews; co-operation was an expected element of their work and it was, in general, freely given. No member of staff refused to participate but their presence or absence from arranged focus group meetings, their degree of participation or non-return of questionnaires all proved acceptable forms of non-co-operation. I was pleasantly surprised that all the obstetricians agreed to be interviewed, albeit some did so reluctantly. Only one doctor proved very reserved, offering minimal input; several 'used' the interview for other purposes, such as having a moan about something different, whilst the majority appeared to value the opportunity to discuss the issues in some detail. Such responses would suggest that enabling individuals to discuss their thoughts about the 'change situation' offers a positive ethical dimension to the process – or conversely, not to include it in the evaluation could be considered unethical.

There is also the consideration of the changing nature of ethnographic research. My work was initially envisaged as a study of the implementation of a radical service development with a focus on the change process, but it has developed more into a study of the nature of midwifery and the influence of the organisation on care delivery. In recognition that the focus might change from that originally intended I negotiated consent from participants on a relatively broad basis, but I was concerned as to whether this constitutes true 'informed' consent. Perhaps a 'process of consent', as described by Munhall (1991) in recognition of this situation, is more appropriate.

Informed consent also requires that the participant be made aware of any potential negative effects that may affect them. In qualitative studies, where it is difficult to entirely anonymise situations, damage to reputations could result from ensuing publications. Thus, in my study, the theoretical analyses, the form of the PhD thesis and subsequent publications will need to be sensitively handled.

Another major area of consideration relates to the possibilities of secondary analysis, whereby data collected for one study is used by other researchers for other purposes. Secondary analysis is becoming an increasingly important strategy for teaching about research as it helps avoid small-scale fieldwork studies, undertaken as part of a course requirement, which can overload RECs and potentially 'contaminate' the research field. Although this may be viewed as a highly appropriate use of a valuable resource, there is an issue about whether anonymity negates the requirement for participants' consent. In recognition of the increasing reuse of data, the Economic and Social Research Council (ESRC) has developed a form that contains different levels of consent for qualitative data collection; participants agree initially to the primary study and again for the data to be stored for secondary analysis.

CONFIDENTIALITY

The assurance of confidentiality through anonymity is another central principle of ethical research in the belief that participants should not be harmed in any way by the research, for example by an individual's views becoming public knowledge, and that they will respond more openly and honestly if they cannot be identified from the data.

Case studies, ethnographies and action research are complex because they are often situation-specific and even sometimes individual-specific. With the current imperative to publish both the evaluations of clinical service developments and research undertaken by practitioners within their own clinical area, these issues are of particular relevance as total anonymity cannot be assured and may not be desirable. Lathlean, in writing about her study of ward sisters, describes how her adherence to the maintenance of confidentiality resulted in a report that was deemed bland by one of the participants, where some of the essence of the situation was lost (Lathlean, 1996b).

Where studies focus on innovative developments, the requirement for total anonymity may be inappropriate. Identification of the study-site, as opposed to the names of individuals, is helpful for units seeking recognition for their work and other service providers attempting to address similar situations. Obviously each study is unique and specific arrangements need to be negotiated with the managers. As my research is part of a large-scale evaluation of a high-profile development, concealing the study-site in material presented in the professional press is impractical and I have sought and received permission for the site to be identified.

Maintaining the anonymity of individuals it more critical as the potential for damage is very real, the researcher and participant's reputations both being at stake. Issues of confidentiality arise at two levels: handling the primary data and making the findings public. The most useful data will be obtained when participants feel assured their responses will be confidential; questionnaires identified by code rather than name and the use of private rooms for interviews can be reassuring but wise respondents may seek reassurance about the subsequent handling of the data.

Since personal interviews were a major source of data for my work and this material was potentially very sensitive, I had to define a clear strategy for handling it. The majority of individual interviews were taped as this enabled me to engage more deeply with the interviewee and ensured an accurate record of their views was used in the subsequent analysis. However, transcribing tapes is a lengthy process, particularly by untrained researchers, and the use of in-house clerical assistance could breach confidentiality. Thus, once completed, the tapes were stored and the transcription undertaken off-site, thereby minimising the chance of voice recognition by a colleague.

Although the transcripts can technically be anonymised by substituting names with codes, the content may clearly identify the speaker. In view of this, if other people handle the material, for example to check coding categories or to verify analyses, they need to be selected with care. An advantage of having the study registered for a higher degree is the access to academic supervision distanced from the health services. For this reason, I negotiated with participants that access to the transcriptions was limited to myself as researcher and my university supervisors, with material only being presented to a 'public' arena in a collated format.

PUBLICATION

When writing for publication, in the majority of instances, individuals' identities can be protected within the presentation of basic demographic data about age, sex, position etc, and their responses hidden within collated formats or presented as variations on a theme. The situation becomes more problematic when reporting issues that relate to a few specific people, for example the actions or reactions of the Clinical Director or Senior Midwifery Manager – individuals who, although not named, can be immediately recognised by readers familiar with the situation. This is particularly relevant to studies such as mine conducted on high-profile developments. However, this attitude does presuppose compromising or negative reporting; in highly successful developments individuals may welcome the publicity, particularly if they feel they have some control over the presentation.

Apart from action research, where the feedback loop is integral to the research approach, and some forms of interactive case study design, the usual aim is to minimise the effect of the research on the study area. Nevertheless, this may not necessarily be appropriate in health service research where it could be considered unethical not to feed back particular concerns as they are identified. Also, closely involving participants at all stages of the work, for example by frequent feedback and discussion about issues as they become apparent, helps to avoid unexpected disclosures at the end. This allows those studied to become active participants rather than passive subjects so that they maintain some sense of control, even ownership of the study. The concept may be difficult for the researcher but, if handled carefully, this approach could enhance their understanding of the situation studied as well as constitute a highly ethical approach.

As my study involved a change process aimed at improving client care feedback was fundamental. This was done on an informal basis as a member of the team overseeing the project implementation and evaluation, for example by highlighting particular concerns raised by specific groups, clarifying positions where some confusion was apparent, or outlining different perspectives on recognised problem areas. This also proved useful to my work as in so doing I gained an understanding of the responses of the managers overseeing the implementation.

As the final analyses of the study are still ongoing I have avoided writing for the professional press to date. However, I am extremely aware of the requirement for sensitive reporting. It would appear only courteous as well as ethical that anything intended for publication where the study site was identified be sent to the unit, as well as to individuals who might be compromised, to confirm acceptability of the proposed publication. One of the unexpected advantages inherent in the delays experienced with this work relates to the time factor – situations change rapidly and the movement of individuals within the NHS can help to confuse identities.

OWNERSHIP

Finally, the end of a project presents yet another ethical dilemma which relates to the ownership of data and who has ultimate control over its use, either for immediate publication or future access. There are some rules of thumb but these are not without their problems. For example, studies undertaken for government departments remain the property of the department but this can lead to the findings being suppressed if they are not in line with policy, for example, The Black Report (Townsend and Davidson, 1982). The trust, funders and researchers may consider they all have some degree of ownership of, and therefore control over, data gathered for evaluations of service development.

Trusts have a particular interest in the findings and may attempt to alter or suppress negative results, or they may plan to use the data for purposes other than originally intended. Some funding bodies have no interest in owning the data of studies they have supported, merely requiring acknowledgement of their support. It is the researcher, who has undertaken the work, who may feel the greatest sense of responsibility to the participants and wish to avoid potential harm by retaining control over the material gathered. Studies developed from evaluations and subsequently registered for a higher degree may present situations of particular confusion. In many instances the position is clear cut, but it is wise to clarify any misunderstanding prior to commencement of the work.

SUPERVISOR'S COMMENTS
Professor Judith Lathlean

Trudy Stevens has described in detail the range of ethical considerations that are important, not only for higher degree research, but also for any research within the health and social care arena. She has illustrated how she has put into practice the principles and how she has tackled the dilemmas. An additional and interesting perspective has been the fact that her PhD work forms part of a much bigger research study. This in itself has its advantages but also its challenges. For example, the research site was already 'chosen' and she did not have to negotiate 'cold' access. However, it potentially places more constraints on the study and such aspects as the ownership of the data.

In much higher degree research, the data automatically 'belongs' to the student researcher and she or he can, within reason, decide on how it is used both within and without the research process.

Some may feel that Trudy was 'lucky' in that it was not deemed necessary for her to go through the whole process of gaining ethics approval although, as she descibes, she did approach the committee. Current MPhil/PhD students are not so fortunate! The norm is for all studies to be submitted to at least one committee and sometimes more than one, for example, both the university where the student is registered and an NHS committee. This has been further complicated by the introduction of regional Medical Research Ethics Committees (MRECs). These are committees (one per region) which have been introduced by the Department of Health, specifically to consider the ethical considerations of national research studies. It is a requirement that all studies wishing to use five or more sites be submitted for approval to an MREC. The idea is that it obviates the necessity to apply to hundreds of Local Research Ethics Committees (LRECs). Nevertheless, LRECs still see proposals that affect their trusts and constituent organisations, in order to consider local issues. The major implication of this is one of time. If MPhil/PhD students are needing to gain permission from more than one LREC, especially if they must consult an MREC, then several months should be allowed for the process. It can be enormously time consuming and may hold up the proceedings of the research.

In addition, some universities require a fairly detailed research proposal to be submitted to a research committee (as opposed to an ethics committee) prior to the student being accepted into the higher degree programme, or for MPhil/PhD registration. When developing their proposals, students are strongly advised to consult one of the several guidelines produced by professional bodies to assist with ensuring ethical research, for example those of the RCN (1993) or the British Psychological Society (1991). This is not only good research practice but is something that both research and ethics committees are looking to see evidence of.

Ensuring that higher degree research is conducted ethically is a potential minefield especially as, unlike in Trudy's case, much higher degree research is not undertaken as part of a larger study. Supervisors should be vigilant at every stage of the work and advise accordingly. However, ultimately it is the student's responsibility to ensure that not only are the formal procedures in place, but also the myriad of other concerns are addressed such as the appropriate use of scarce resources and, within health care, the conduct of research that will, at least in the long term, be for the benefit of better client, consumer and patient care.

REFERENCES

British Psychological Society (1991) *Code of Conduct, Ethical Principles and Guidelines*. Leicester: British Psychological Society.

Buckingham, S. (1996) Watching me watching you: dilemmas in pain assessment of children. In: De Raeve, L. (ed.) *Nursing Research: An Ethical and Legal Appraisal*. London: Baillière Tindall.

Department of Health (1993) *Changing Childbirth: Report of the Expert Maternity Group. Part 1*. London: HMSO.

Ersser, S. (1996) Ethnography in clinical situations: an ethical appraisal. In: De Raeve, L. (ed.) *Nursing Research: an Ethical and Legal Appraisal*. London: Baillière Tindall.

Goffman, E. (1959) *The Presentation of Self in Everyday Life*. Harmondsworth: Penguin Books.

Hammersley, M. (1992) *What's Wrong with Ethnography?* London: Routledge.

Homan, R. (1991) *The Ethics of Social Research*. Harlow: Longman.

Lathlean, J. (1996a) Ethical dimensions of action research. In: De Raeve, L. (ed.) *Nursing Research: An Ethical and Legal Appraisal*. London: Baillière Tindall.

Lathlean, J. (1996b) Ethical issues for nursing research: a methodological focus. *Nursing Times Research;* 1: 3, 175–183.

Lipson, J.G. (1991) The use of self in ethnographic research. In: Morse, J.M. (ed.) *Qualitative Nursing Research: A Contemporary Dialogue*. London: Sage.

McCourt, C., Page, L. (eds.) (1996) *Report on the Evaluation of One-to-One Midwifery Practice*. London: Thames Valley University.

Munhall, P.L. (1991) Institutional Review of Qualitative Research Proposals. In: J.M. (ed.) *Qualitative Nursing Research: A Contemporary Dialogue*. London: Sage.

Pickering, N. (1996) Ethical review of nursing research. In: De Raeve, L. (ed.) *Nursing Research: An Ethical and Legal Appraisal*. London: Baillière Tindall.

Polanyi, M. (1967) *The Tacit Dimension*. London: Routledge and Kegan Paul.

Reed, J., Proctor, S. (1995) *Practitioner Research in Health Care: The Inside Story*. London: Chapman and Hall.

Royal College of Nursing Research Advisory Group (1993) *Ethics Related to Research in Nursing*. London: Royal College of Nursing.

Tierney, A. (1995) The role of research ethics committees. In: *Nurse Researcher: Ethical Issues in Research;* 3: 1, 43–52.

Townsend, P. and Davidson, N. (1982) *Inequalities in Health: The Black Report*. Harmondsworth: Penguin.

Young, M. (1991) *An Inside Job*. Oxford: Clarendon Press.

4. Interdisciplinary research: a consideration of some key issues

Author
Owen Barr

Commentary
Rob Millar

INTRODUCTION

Several commentators have noted the need for increased interdisciplinary research projects in nursing and other health care professions and there is growing recognition of the need for interdisciplinary research projects among researchers and funding agencies (Lorentzon, 1995; Mackenzie et al., 1995; Ross and Meerabeau, 1997; Read, 1998). Within this context it is reasonable to anticipate that a growing number of nurses and students from other areas of health and social care will engage in interdisciplinary projects during their postgraduate studies.

Interdisciplinary research projects can range from a collaboration between a postgraduate student and a local service in which the student does the majority of the work. Alternatively it could be a collaboration between a few members of the local primary health care team or hospital services, with little (if any) additional funding. It could also involve several different disciplines, a number of local, national or international sites and significant external funding (with the associated management structures).

Interdisciplinary research projects have the potential to provide more comprehensive answers to research questions, however, like all projects this approach is not without challenges to be overcome. Through reflecting primarily on the process of completing an MSc in Guidance and Counselling that sought to gain insight into parents' expectations and experiences of receiving genetic counselling, this chapter explores some of the key issues which people undertaking interdisciplinary research may find it helpful to consider. Several of the issues raised also have implications for other forms of collaborative research, for example between similar professionals within the same or from different services.

Most research questions can be traced back to an earlier experience or interest of the researcher. This project, like most, had a long gestational period. An interest in genetic counselling arose from a series of encounters (as a community nurse for people with learning disabilities) with some parents as they prepared for genetic counselling. It appeared that they tried to balance an excitement that they may receive positive information that their new child will have a positive future and further children will be healthy, with the concern that this may not be so and any further children may have an inherited condition. It appeared to me that these anticipated appointments were very different for parents than the various other appointments they regularly attended. While I always tried to provide parents with what 'I thought' to be relevant information and support, I was also conscious over a period of several years that I was possibly missing 'something' about the significance of their expectations and experiences.

Recent years have seen a growing interest in the potential of genetics to explain and possibly reduce the incidence of a range of childhood disabilities. Whist accepting this, less attention is given to the need to further understand the process of genetic counselling and the personal experiences of parents (Marteau and Richards, 1996). This nagging uncertainty that I regularly tossed around in my head about the process of genetic counselling eventually matured into the research question in an MSc Guidance and Counselling course. The long process of maturation paid dividends when the frustration and pressure mounted during the process of completing the project, as it is easier to sustain the considerable investment of the personal energy and commitment necessary at difficult times if the researcher feels strongly about the topic.

THE NATURE OF INTERDISCIPLINARY RESEARCH

Bringing together a range of different professionals to consider a research question is recognition of the interrelated variables that can affect outcomes of professional interventions. It is argued that the collaboration of people from differing disciplines with their corresponding differences in values, histories, politics, culture, language, methodological philosophies, approaches and analytical procedures will enhance the validity and applicability to practice of the knowledge generated (Ross, 1996). This aim is evident within several recently published interdisciplinary research projects (Thomas and Graver, 1997; Wright et al, 1997; Bennett, 1998).

Ambler (1997) emphasised the potential of interdisciplinary research to successfully combine academic and practice-focused approaches. The pooling of knowledge, skills, previous experience and motivation has also been reported to lead to a number of additional advantages. These include the development of increased formal as well as informal research and practice orientated networks that can lead to people involved developing new knowledge and skills. Assistance with access to potential participants for difficult studies and access to a greater number of research funding opportunities may result from interdisciplinary collaboration. The end result can be a greater degree of acceptance of the researchers, the project and its findings across a wider range of health and social care professionals (Mackenzie et al, 1995;

Ambler, 1997; Bennett, 1998). This point is further highlighted by the need for nurses to undertake research that contributes not only to the development of nursing knowledge but is also sufficiently robust that it contributes to the wider body of health care research (Rafferty and Traynor, 1997).

It is important that the ethos of interdisciplinary working is evident throughout the research process and does not become a superficial exercise in which a few professionals are added to the research team in order that access to further funding opportunities may be increased. Effective interdisciplinary research is more than nurses assisting in other professionals' projects; Ross and Meerabeau (1997) have highlighted the need for methodological pluralism and caution against a superficial approach to interdisciplinary research. They stressed the fact that successful interdisciplinary research is 'a difficult intellectual and often emotionally demanding task of listening carefully to the unfamiliar scientific territory of researchers from a different background and working to integrate these ideas into the design, analysis and reporting of studies'. Mastering this task requires a considerable degree of confidence in one's qualities as a person and abilities as a professional, if one is to become an effective interdisciplinary researcher.

INTERDISCIPLINARY RESEARCH — SOME NOTES OF CAUTION

The need for interdisciplinary research appears to be generally accepted, but several areas of caution about developments in this area have also emerged. These can be considered within two main categories, broadly separated into professional and personal issues.

Professional issues

A major concern repeatedly expressed relates to the perceived dominance of the medical approach to research (Ross and Meerabeau, 1997; Casey and Hoy, 1997; Rafferty and Traynor, 1997). It has been argued that an uneven playing field exists in relation to accessing research funding, with the major share going to medical scientific orientated research. This perceived differential in research methods in turn places qualitative designs, often associated with nurses, other therapists and social scientists at a disadvantage (Ambler, 1997; Casey and Hoy, 1997). There is evidence in the acceptance by some funding committees of randomised control trials as the 'gold standard' in research designs. This design has been strongly challenged by Rolfe (1998) who contends that the reliance on statistical significance in findings of random control trials leads to a utilitarian perspective of 'the greatest good for the greatest number'. It is a position that he feels strongly is ethically incompatible with individualised holistic nursing care. Similar views have been expressed by Lorentzon (1995) who highlights the risk that nurses will be 'seduced' by the attraction of additional research funding and increased recognition that may come from adopting a purely quantitative scientific research design. She asserts that while nurses should recognise the contribution this approach may have, they should continue to value their own research perspectives.

A further challenge to effective interdisciplinary research may arise from the assumption by doctors or other more 'senior' professionals that they should be the 'de facto' leaders of the project. This may result in a superficial appearance of interdisciplinary research when in reality it is a medically controlled venture from development to dissemination and as such fails to meet the major challenges of integrated approaches required for successful interdisciplinary research (Ross and Meerabeau, 1997).

Personal issues

Some professionals engaging in interdisciplinary research may perceive an increased risk of professional and personal embarrassment. This may arise from the need to outline and in some instances defend previous research approaches; the need to negotiate the proposed research question; and attempts to or resistance against the integration of a variety of perspectives into the research project (Mackenzie et al, 1995). Researchers as people and as professionals, including students, may have individual sensitivities that must be acknowledged and carefully responded to. These could relate to their own assumptions about their role in the project, their professional background, an actual or perceived position in a hierarchy, or personal characteristics such as age, gender and academic qualifications (Lorentzon, 1998).

Inherent in the preceding issues is the possibility that individuals may have competing agendas for their involvement in interdisciplinary research. This can result in a desire to be involved in only some aspects of the project, for example, those with a high profile such as launches, awards and publications. However, they may be less interested in the more time-consuming aspects of instrument development, data collection and analysis. Without regular contact between those involved it is likely that the few people who stay most involved will fashion the design and implementation of the research. Consequently the interdisciplinary understanding is reduced and this may result in fragmentation and disagreement between people at a later stage, for example during data analysis. In essence interdisciplinary research projects require individuals who possess the qualities, knowledge and skills of a collaborative team member (Hennemann et al, 1995), who are willing and able to engage in the difficult task of developing an integrated research design.

If effective collaboration is absent, different degrees of direct and indirect censorship may occur. This can manifest itself in failure to be granted funding or ethical permission for a proposed project, or the deliberate hindering of an approved project by placing restrictions on access to participants or the instruments that may be used. Even if the project is completed some degree of censorship may still occur through the refusal to accept articles that report on the project for presentation at key conferences or in particular publications (Mason, 1997; Rolfe, 1998).

LIMITED GUIDANCE

Despite the growing interest it appears that little has been written on the processes leading to successful interdisciplinary research. Mackenzie et al, (1995) reported a lack of 'authoritative guidance' for people considering the development of collaborative research projects that would guide them through the 'complex matrix of interactions (between individuals and institutions) that are a common feature of interdisciplinary commissioned research'.

The remainder of this chapter uses the five-phase framework for the research process outlined by Polit and Hungler (1997) to discuss the measures that may be taken to increase the prospects of successful interdisciplinary research collaboration. Following an exploration of the key aspects involved each section will conclude with a summary of the practical steps taken in the completion of a MSc in Guidance and Counselling. While these are specific to one project undertaken, they provide real examples of the issues that can arise and possible responses.

THE CONCEPTUAL PHASE

Communication between people

A major influence in the success of interdisciplinary collaboration in service provision and research is effective communication between the people involved (Ovretveit, 1993; Bennett, 1998). Relationships between people develop over time as the individuals involved become aware of the abilities of their collaborators, as well as gain insight into the professional and personal agendas that may exist. The development of increased self-awareness is important in helping prospective researchers to recognise how their behaviour and the manner in which they interact with other people could impact on the development and maintenance of collaborative relationships.

Negotiating possible research questions

Most researchers, irrespective of the academic level of their study, have specific ideas about questions that they would like to investigate. From this starting point prospective researchers further refine their question and clarify the limits of their study. Students engaging in an interdisciplinary project must acknowledge a range of perspectives arising from other people involved when refining research questions. During initial meetings with potential collaborators it is necessary to balance enthusiasm and commitment to undertake interdisciplinary research with a willingness to discuss amendments to the manner in which the research could be undertaken. A potential difficulty with the research questions in the MSc project was that they might have been viewed as evaluating the services provided by staff in the Department of Medical Genetics. This possible interpretation was acknowledged but any limited concerns about it were outweighed by the opportunity to gain further insight into the perspective of parents.

The facilitation of opportunities to discuss how different perspectives may be integrated to form a coherent research question, or series of questions, is an important aspect of developing relationships between the people involved. This is best organised as a planned meeting with established start and finish times, rather than always trying to catch 10 or 15 spare minutes with someone. In the early stages of an interdisciplinary research study, potential collaborators are likely to be engaged to some degree in assessing the abilities and competence of each other. Every opportunity should be taken by students to demonstrate competence in skills essential for successful partnerships, such as interpersonal communication skills, synthesis of ideas, presentation of information and time management.

As the discussions move from broad ideas about research to more specific research topics and possible research questions students must be careful to remain clear about their topic and preferred approach. The supervisor is an important sounding board in this process and they have a major role to undertake in keeping students focused on the project in hand.

Getting people 'on board'

In current health and social care services, time and other resources are at a premium and therefore it is often necessary to 'prove' the case to new potential partners as to why they should invest time in an interdisciplinary project. An important strategy in this is clarifying how the proposed research may assist the clients of the overall service and the potential professional, academic and personal advantages for collaborators. These messages could be enhanced through the provision of written information to colleagues. Such information should be accurate, supported by up-to-date literature, be presented in a neat folder and contain contact information in case anyone wishes to discuss it further.

It is worth investing time in identifying potential partners on the basis of common interests and complementary skills, and actively seeking out like-minded people, rather than simply teaming up with other people because they are local. The required information may be obtained from publications on the proposed research area. In addition much of this information is now available on university websites which often list research interests and publications of staff. Owing to advances in electronic communication such as fax machines, e-mail, telephone and video conferencing it is now easier to bring together interdisciplinary research teams previously separated by geographical obstacles.

During this phase it is necessary to carefully plan out a general direction for the project and tentatively agree practical issues including: who the main researcher(s) would be; the level of support expected from each researcher; ownership of data; and authorship rights of any publications that arise from the research. Lack of investment in these earlier discussions can result in vagueness about the nature of the research and can lead to confusion over the most effective way forward. To avoid this, the action plan which I instigated prior to my research is shown in Table 1.

Table 1. Practical steps taken during the conceptual phase

▶ Potential research area and tentative questions were developed in Year 2 of PG Dip (five months before expected registration date for MSc). Previous areas of study and interests from nursing practice influenced these.

▶ Potential collaborators were identified, mindful of the contribution they could make in helping to provide a holistic answer to the research question on the basis of previous experience and informal network.

▶ Initial meetings were set up three months prior to expected date of registration for MSc to discuss possible collaboration between interested parties.

▶ Time available for meetings was confirmed and opportunities facilitated for all potential partners to contribute.

▶ I listened actively at meetings and remained alert for individual strengths and sensitivities of potential partners. Particular interests of staff were identified and concerns noted in relation to proposed research aims and objectives.

▶ Possible amendments to the general direction and limits of the research project were negotiated.

▶ The degree of commitment required from prospective collaborators was explained.

▶ The need for ethical approval and from whom this may be obtained was discussed.

▶ Contact information was exchanged with all potential collaborators to stimulate the development of research networks.

▶ Meetings were discussed with Course Director (research supervisor not yet appointed).

▶ All discussions were accurately recorded for my own notes, giving specific reference to any undertaking to complete any additional tasks outside of the meeting.

DESIGN AND PLANNING PHASE

This phase is perhaps the most demanding in the interdisciplinary research process as it is necessary to agree the nature of the overall research design that accommodates the perspectives of the interdisciplinary researchers involved in the project. If the general ethos and core values of the project have been agreed in earlier meetings during the conceptual phase, the process of discussion and integration of various perspectives will be smoother, although rarely 'pain free'.

The finalised research aims and objectives need to be agreed early in this stage, as these will inform the design and planning of the project and will have a major influence on the collaborators who will be involved in the project. Students should discuss the proposed aims and objectives with their research supervisor to confirm the degree to which these fit with what is required for this particular level of study. A risk with interdisciplinary projects is that after discussion with colleagues, during which each one may add a little bit on, the project becomes unnecessarily complicated. The research supervisor has a key role to play in keeping the project manageable and within the bounds of what is required for any particular course of study.

Agreeing on possible participants

The combination of researchers involved in the project will also have an influence on the range of participants to be included. Agreement should be reached with all interdisciplinary researchers involved as to the inclusion criteria for participants in the project and any restrictions on overall numbers prior to commencing data collection. Individual researchers should be encouraged to provide their rationale for the boundaries created by the inclusion criteria and thus make them transparent. This is an important step in reducing the influence of alternative professional and personal agendas for inclusion criteria. Significant differences can exist between the number of participants considered necessary for an adequate sample depending on the research aims, objectives, design and plans for analysis. Therefore it is helpful to agree the expected number of participants when finalising the research design, as this will assist and orientate people, including the research supervisor, to the agreed design and finer details of the study.

Gaining access to participants for research studies can be a frustrating process and normally involves the need to obtain permission from a variety of agencies who hold confidential information about prospective participants (for example, clinic lists, appointment times, home addresses). Seidman (1991) asserts that gaining access to participants is a 'crucial feature' of research and should be undertaken personally. Setting up meetings with key people can facilitate this process, and it is useful to anticipate possible questions about the nature and remit of the study, the likely use of findings and to provide this information with the initial request for access. Remember that employers and other agencies can only provide access to participants; you must then obtain informed consent from participants to join the study.

A specific difficulty that can arise when trying to get access to collect data from staff of any service is finding out to whom the request for assistance should go. If the letters are sent too high up in the organisation it increases the time before you get a response. Conversely if the letters go too low in the organisation it may offend the sensitivities of some managers and lead to some degree of direct or indirect censorship. An advantage of local interdisciplinary research is that other team members may have different networks through which to access participants. A further advantage of having interdisciplinary collaboration is that it may assist in gaining additional insights into variables to consider when deciding how to recruit participants. Other researchers may have encountered previous difficulties and have developed solutions. All in all, recruiting people to a project can be a long and complicated process.

The nature of measurement

Once again negotiation is necessary. The decisions on the nature of data collection are central to the project and need to be discussed at length. It may be possible to use or adapt existing instruments that can then be piloted and validated for the purpose of a specific project. However, it may be necessary to design new instruments/strategies that could be quantitative or qualitative in nature. The remit of the instrument should therefore be established, together with areas to be included and some indication of the length of time required for participants to provide information. Following initial discussions students should prepare a draft instrument to be circulated to potential collaborators. This can be adapted on the basis of feedback received, but ultimately the student must finalise and defend any instrument used in the study. This may involve some negotiation with collaborators in an attempt to reach an agreed format. It is important that all people involved accept the structure and content of plans for data collection as this will form the basis for analysis and influence confidence in subsequent findings. Students should carefully record details of this process as it could support the reliability of the instrument developed.

This phase defines the structures from which the project will be built. It can be particularly intellectually and emotionally demanding as it may be the first time you have needed to explain and defend your plans to other professionals (Ross and Meerabeau, 1997). Their feedback can be mixed and it is most useful to view their comments as constructive suggestions to be considered, rather than major criticisms to be totally rejected or absolute requests that must be followed.

Several recent projects have reported that an action research approach worked well in bringing a range of professionals to a common understanding (Thomas and Graver, 1997; Bennett, 1998). The development of a triangulated research design that incorporates both quantitative and qualitative aspects can prove a useful compromise. Particular consideration should be given to the style of language and words used, as it is possible that across team members similar words have different meanings and vice versa (Casey and Hoy, 1997).

It is necessary to remain alert to individual, professional and personal sensitivities when discussing aspects of measurement, particularly if the desire is to evaluate aspects of service. This can be especially difficult if too narrow a location is selected within a specialist area of services; for example, if only one clinic or other type of service exists in the study area it may be possible for people to identify specific service staff or possibly clients of the service. Therefore, with specialist projects care must be taken to protect the anonymity of participants and staff providing the service.

Gaining ethical approval

All research projects have ethical considerations, although not all require approval from the Research Ethics Committee (see Chapter 3). As criteria for requiring approval can vary across different settings, all students should check with their supervisor if their proposed project requires approval. It is preferable to ask questions and have it confirmed that no permission is necessary, rather than have a project delayed or halted due to the lack of approval.

In an interdisciplinary research project it is possible that more than one committee needs to receive a submission. If at all possible, agree with colleagues on a primary committee to approach – this will normally require some discussion and could lead to disagreement about which committee is the most important. Reaching a clear agreement about this will reduce the likelihood of further conflict that may jeopardise permission to gain access to participants later. Challenges to effective interdisciplinary research will arise occasionally, for instance when another professional group feels it is unnecessary to submit a proposal to one researcher's committee but then expects colleagues to submit a proposal to 'their' committee. The development of interdisciplinary proposals consistent with the ethos of the project is desirable and individual ethical submissions should be avoided where possible. A student will normally have to get approval from their university Research Ethics Committee (REC), although approval by another committee may be accepted. The student should confirm this in writing prior to commencing their data collection.

Once approval has been received from this committee it may be possible to have this accepted as adequate by other relevant groups. However it may not be this straightforward and additional submissions to other committees may be necessary. Timing is crucial with respect to applying for ethics approval as committees meet with varying frequencies across different areas. Therefore students should obtain the necessary forms and a calendar of committee meetings early in the planning of the project.

Among many students and other researchers an REC can be associated with an air of mystique and thus generate concerns about projects being judged as right or wrong, good or bad. This may result in the design of projects in such as way as to not require ethical approval, for example by not speaking directly with clients. Unfortunately this restricts the project's remit and may result in important insights not being explored. It is more useful to view committees as playing a very important role in facilitating the development of ethically sound projects that respect the rights of potential participants and offer advice and guidance to researchers. In this way they become an integral and positive part of the research process rather than another obstacle to overcome.

RECs may request additional information and points of clarification or the committee may place restrictions on the original design of a project. When this occurs it will be necessary to decide how best to retain the interdisciplinary research process while keeping the focus on the agreed aims, objectives and design. If suggested changes are considerable then it will be necessary to agree amendments that would be acceptable to the researchers involved or possibly review the feasibility of the project continuing in its present form.

In my case following feedback from the REC (in respect of the MSc outlined in Table 2) it was necessary to alter the pathway by which potential participants would be contacted and return their consent form if they agreed to participate. It was also necessary to make more specific statements in the introductory letter about confidentiality and anonymity for participants. Further to this, the committee asked if a small-scale project as proposed (10–15 people) was sufficient for an MSc dissertation – the supervisor confirmed that this was acceptable. The necessary changes were agreed with all involved in the project and a prompt reply sent to the REC who then confirmed approval for the project. The need to undertake further work on the basis of feedback can lead to frustration which may be compounded by delays that can result from the need to get in touch with colleagues to discuss issues raised by the REC. Viewing the comments of the committee in the light they were offered, that is to improve your project, often provides the encouragement needed to deal promptly with the issues raised.

Owing to the possibility of requests for further information or requested changes, students with deadlines for submission should consider undertaking the majority of the preliminary work and submitting a proposal for ethical approval either prior to or very shortly after registering for their dissertation. While this requires an additional investment of time (possibly during the summer prior to registration) and will normally need access to staff at the university, it has the advantage of making you consider in detail the nature of your project, its design and the development of the instruments. This in turn reduces the risk of needing to make major changes later in the project when time is at a significant premium.

A note on potential publications

For many people the end of a project and any possible publications appears a long way off during the planning and design phase, but in reality it may only be a few months to a year away. It is therefore important to give some consideration at this early stage to the possibility of publication and some pertinent issues related to this. An agreement should be reached that provides guidance on the authorship of papers and criteria for the ordering of names. It is generally accepted that the student should be first author of articles reporting data from their research. This can be a particular issue when those involved are subject to appraisals and exercises such as the Research Assessment Exercise (RAE) in which the numbers of their publications have wider implications for their career progression. It is essential that these guidelines establish if anyone has a right of veto to the presentation of information or just have to receive a copy of submitted papers, but do not necessarily have to agree with their content. Thinking through issues at this stage will reduce the likelihood of difficulties at a later stage. Students should discuss these issues with their supervisor before finalising any agreement. My second stage action plan ensured that all collaborators were as involved as possible – see Table 2.

Table 2. Practical steps taken during design and planning phase

▶ I ensured all initial undertakings completed within agreed timescale, or relevant people informed of reason for and length of any expected delay.

▶ I finalised research aims and objectives with research supervisor and staff and Department of Medical Genetics. This involved a reduction in the initial proposed number of participants and a widening of inclusion criteria.

▶ The limits of the literature review were established; this was guided by a clearer focus on the research question and discussion with supervisor.

▶ The use of a triangulated approach was confirmed, involving the combined use of questionnaires and interviews to collect data.

▶ The three data collection points were agreed and copies of the proposed instruments were provided to staff at Department of Medical Genetics.

▶ The procedure for providing letters to potential participants was agreed.

▶ Information was prepared for application to the university Research Ethics Committee. Agreement was reached that Consultant would be named as supporting the project. Forms were discussed with Course Director and generally agreed that the project was practical.

▶ A submission was made to the university Research Ethics Committee at the earliest possible opportunity. This was October 1997, three weeks after registering for MSc. This was only possible due to the preparatory work that had been completed in the previous three months.

▶ Amendments required by university Research Ethics Committee were discussed and alterations agreed. Following a prompt response to the university Research Ethics Committee, ethical approval was granted.

▶ Initial discussion on possibility of publications and how these might be organised.

▶ Introductory letters and consent form were prepared for staff at Department of Medical Genetics and recruitment of participants commenced.

▶ Contacts were made with other researchers in the area. This was as a result of their names appearing in literature and through informal networks. E-mail was main means of contact.

THE EMPIRICAL (DATA COLLECTION) PHASE

Data collection can be particularly time consuming, especially when it involves several data collection points in a longitudinal design, a large geographical distribution of participants and detailed interviews. Although not foreseen by some students, a frequent challenge which often arises is to gain and maintain the participants' co-operation over the period of data collection. Participants may be suspicious of the project, the researchers, and what will be done with the data; these concerns may not arise until they become aware of the detail included in the questions. They may well have seen it all before and have had little reward for their previous participation in research. All participants should have been provided with adequate information to make an informed decision about their involvement. None the less it may be necessary to discuss this information further or provide additional information in the course of data collection.

While it appears to have little recognition in the research literature, it is important to acknowledge the frustration associated with falling numbers of participants. Students can sometimes become anxious about their project evaporating and being left with inadequate data to complete their course. Such concerns should be discussed with the research supervisor and reassurance sought about the most appropriate strategies to use. Temptations to alter aspects of the project can arise, for example, rewording the introductory letter to be more 'encouraging' about participating and less open about feeling free not to participate. Other options include sending further reminder letters than those agreed in the design phase, widening the sample to increase numbers or using other strategies to increase the total of participants. Whilst it may be necessary to amend aspects of the project as it is being implemented, these amendments should be discussed with interdisciplinary colleagues, where necessary, the REC. If changes are made without appropriate support, adequate numbers may be recruited but in the process the findings of the project may be invalidated including those obtained from the legitimate participants. It is better to defend smaller numbers with strict procedures than higher numbers with inappropriate methods.

During this phase it is important to maintain contact with colleagues and provide regular updates in respect of progress and difficulties encountered, as well as provide and receive encouragement. Such contact provides opportunities to discuss any need for amendments to the previous design in light of experiences gained during data collection. It is also important to use time during data collection to complete the earlier parts of the research report/

dissertation instead of leaving it all to do at the end in a major rush. If students take opportunities when time is available to work on earlier sections of the final document this provides the opportunity to reflect on this material and refine it before final submission – rather than finding oneself working against the clock and then submitting earlier less refined thoughts and conclusions.

Careful recording and filing is essential to ensure that no data are lost, as this could have major practical and ethical implications, such as incomplete data sets or breaches of confidentiality. It is advisable to have the basis of the recording system developed and ready to run before the first data is collected. Leaving it until you have some data increases the risk that they may be misplaced in the hectic schedule associated with additional data collection. Effective recording assists in keeping track of progress made and work yet to be completed. This can provide reinforcement of efforts and at the same time keep students within their timetable.

Table 3. Practical steps taken during the empirical (data collection) phase

▶ Questionnaires were sent to, and interviews arranged with, participants on receipt of a completed consent form.

▶ The agreed procedure for sending one reminder letter was maintained, despite a slow response rate for questionnaires.

▶ I kept accurate records of dates when questionnaires were sent and returned and the details of interviews.

▶ I discussed the low return rate of questionnaires between Time 1 and Time 2 with supervisor and was reassured that adequate numbers were being returned. The emphasis on the need for strict procedures rather than large numbers was reinforced.

▶ Regular contact with staff at the Department of Medical Genetics was kept up to remain up to date with the number of people being seen at clinics and whether any particular difficulties had arisen as a result of the project.

▶ Questionnaire data was coded and logged for analysis each week in order to prevent a build-up.

▶ Introduction and literature review chapters were revised in preparation for final submission.

▶ Contact details were provided to participants in case they wished to further discuss the research project.

▶ I confirmed which parents wished to have a summary of findings sent to them.

THE ANALYSIS PHASE

I found this phase required clear planning of time available to undertake the analysis and consider the results. It was necessary to spend blocks of time working with data in order that interrelationships became apparent and often material was revisited on a number of occasions. Analysis cannot be undertaken effectively by doing it in a disjointed manner in 'spare' time. It was therefore necessary to give priority to this task and consequently other work and additional projects had to take second place. Students should look forward in the timescale of the project and block out time for the analysis to be undertaken. This may mean completing other work sooner than expected, delaying other work or not accepting any additional non-essential tasks.

The process of analysis is undertaken in order that the questions within the research aims and objectives can be answered. The increasing sophistication of computer software makes analysis of both quantitative and qualitative data faster (once the software packages have been mastered). Despite these advances in information technology, analysis remains a time-consuming task and in many ways more so in interdisciplinary research. The task of integrating various professional backgrounds, cultures and interpretations into a coherent report can be professionally and personally very challenging (Ross and Meerabeau, 1997).

All data are open to interpretation and the same results, be they quantitative or qualitative in origin, can be interpreted in more ways than one. As noted earlier in the chapter an attraction of interdisciplinary research was bringing together a number of people to develop a more holistic answer. The integration of findings can involve much discussion relating to possible interpretations, which can test the depth of interdisciplinary understanding and willingness to learn from each other. Long-held views about clients, services and other professional groups may be challenged directly and indirectly. Discussion and debate need to be viewed as part and parcel of the interdisciplinary process, an essential component to developing new knowledge and understandings rather than an unfortunate difficulty.

The aim of interdisciplinary research, however, is not to gain unanimous agreement, rather opportunities should exist for alternative interpretations to be presented. Individual sensitivities must be recognised and responded to appropriately. With this in mind alternative interpretations of the findings could be reported to provide readers with the opportunity to reach their own conclusions. Researchers must remain true to the commitment they gave to participants to accurately report their data. Students must keep in close contact with their research supervisor at this stage as they can often provide a more objective opinion. This is because they are not immediately involved in the discussion. Supervisors can also provide valuable advice about how to remain focused on the project and not get caught up with wider service issues.

There is always potential for politics to obstruct accurate and open reporting of research findings (Mason, 1997). Pressure to reduce the focus on a particular aspect of a project (usually negative) and increase it on another (usually positive) may arise from the research group, concerned managers, or from the influence of professional and personal agendas. This pressure can be even more acute if the research has been commissioned for a specific purpose. For these reasons all people collaborating in the research should have the opportunity to discuss draft reports, seek clarifications and discuss possible amendments. The submission of joint reports and publications makes it less likely that censorship against one team member will be effective. It is more defensible to report findings accurately and stimulate debate than it is to amend findings to fit in with individual agendas and so reduce criticism and discussion.

Table 4. Practical steps taken during the analysis phase

- I completed entry of data from questionnaires in preparation for analysis with the Statistical Package for Social Sciences on the PC.
- Tapes were transcribed and content analysis undertaken – a lengthy process involving six or seven hours for each hour on tape.
- Discussions with supervisor and some staff at Department of Medical Genetics about the possible interpretation of findings and qualitative information were held.
- Triangulation of findings was undertaken with specific focus on research aims and objectives.
- Further analysis was undertaken in response to the above discussions in order to clarify key issues raised and check out possible interpretations of findings.
- It was agreed that the report would omit the location of clinics attended as these could possibly lead to the identification of doctors and participants due to specialist nature of the service.
- Attention was given to clarifying the practical implications and recommendations that derived from the findings.

THE DISSEMINATION PHASE

All research projects are major investments by participants, the individual researchers and their organisations, of personal and organisational resources, and it is reasonable for all concerned to expect a return for the investment. A practical return is the effective dissemination of the research findings. Dissemination is the final stage of the research process and not an optional extra. Researchers must actively engage in this process if the findings of their project are to have any hope of influencing practice and become more than an academic exercise that will be confined to a shelf in a university library.

Participants should have the opportunities to access the findings of the study, although practically this may not be possible, for instance when using an anonymously completed instrument, and it is doubtful that participants would want to receive individual copies of the complete report. A range of practical strategies can be used to directly inform groups (for example students, parents groups, voluntary organisations, staff groups) who have participated in the study through seminars and poster presentations in facilities where they work or meet. If interviews have been undertaken participants could be asked if they wish to receive a summary of the findings when they become available. If a copy would be appreciated then an expected timescale should be given for when the results will be ready and a note taken of the address to where these should be posted. This was the format of direct feedback to participants who assisted in the MSc in Guidance and Counselling. Participants were asked at the conclusion of their interview if they wished to receive written feedback, the address to which they wanted this sent was noted and it was explained that this information would be available after the project had been submitted to and marked by the university lecturers.

Research findings should also be made available to other interested parties, such as staff in the services studied, other colleagues and wider statutory/independent services. Even when the researcher feels confident in their findings, providing direct feedback to staff in services can be anxiety-provoking. Concerns can arise for the researcher about whether staff will accept the findings, whether it will become clear that an important aspect of information has been missed or that something could have been interpreted differently if more information had been provided. Balanced against these concerns is the need to obtain feedback on the findings and discuss the practical implications of these if the project is to result in service developments. The findings of the MSc Guidance and Counselling were outlined to staff in the Department of Medical Genetics and key recommendations for the need to develop an information leaflet and review pre- and post-appointment support were explored in a positive manner. Taking time to have these feedback discussions also provides the opportunity to tentatively discuss possible further research projects and how the information gained and lessons learnt in undertaking the initial project could be built upon. In relation to the above project, discussions centred around developing a project at doctorate level in relation to genetic counselling and the provision of personal genetic information. It was possible even at this early stage to discuss possible support for another project and a potential project supervisor and specialist project adviser.

Further to providing direct feedback to participants and staff from services involved, it is useful to explore several other approaches to disseminate findings to a wider audience. These can vary considerably depending on the nature of the project and the findings to be reported. Possible strategies include: high profile launches, press releases and local, national or international conference presentations. Publications in academic and professional journals or newspapers and on Internet sites have the advantage of reaching a wider range of people as well as becoming permanent records that may be accessed by readers at a later date. Publications in journals make it possible to target specific audiences with individually tailored presentations that reflect their concerns.

The effective dissemination of findings, even through a variety of channels is not enough to guarantee change will occur and is discussed fully in Chapter 7. I would like to share (Table 5) the practical steps which I took based on the considerable attitudinal, professional, personal and organisational obstacles to the implementation of research findings (Parahoo, 1998). To increase the chances of the findings having a direct effect on services it is important that the practical implications and possible amendments to services are reported. Recommendations are most useful if they are specific rather than broad (for example develop an information leaflet, rather than increase communication to parents) and the rationale for suggested changes is provided. If at all possible, maintaining contact with services after the research is completed and providing regular encouragement may also facilitate the practical implementation of research findings.

Once again the issue of individual sensitivities must be considered with particular reference to presentations and publications. The earlier agreements on the ownership of data and rights to publish are central to this. Bearing in mind that some people may wish to read the dissertation in full it is important that information is provided on where this can be located.

Enthusiastic research students should remember that recommendations for change might be interpreted as a criticism of current services. In some ways there is no avoiding this conclusion, but it can be influenced by the manner in which recommendations are presented. Balance is essential, and recommendations for development should be built upon existing good practice that was identified in the project.

Table 5. Practical steps taken during the dissemination phase

▶ Feedback meetings were undertaken with key staff from Department of Medical Genetics.

▶ Information was prepared and disseminated to parents who wished to receive a copy – this was five pages long and contained details of where the MSc could be read and contact details if they wished to discuss further any information provided.

▶ I requested feedback from participants on the summary sent to them – this was in the form of responses to some open questions about the findings.

▶ Papers were submitted for local nursing conference and this will be followed by submission of papers to nursing, wider health care and counselling journals and conferences.

▶ Discussion were held with some staff at Department of Medical Genetics about the recommendations for information leaflets and increased local pre- and post-appointment support.

▶ Tentative ideas were presented for doctorate studies to further develop issues arising from the MSc findings, and potential supervisors and advisers were identified.

▶ An outline proposal was refined and currently an application to the Research Ethical Committee is being developed.

CONCLUSION

While debate is likely to continue on the relative merits of interdisciplinary research for nurses, it is clear that this approach has a major contribution to make to wider health care research and nurses should be involved to some degree (Rafferty and Traynor, 1997; Lorentzon, 1998). Irrespective of the pace at which interdisciplinary research emerges as an approach to answer increasingly complex health and social care related questions, specific nursing research will need to continue (Lorentzon, 1998). Interdisciplinary research is an approach to the organisation of research, but not the only way to do it. The key consideration remains how best a specific research question can be answered.

Interdisciplinary research will not occur unassisted and just bringing a group of people interested in research together is no more a guarantee of successful interdisciplinary research than bringing a number of different professionals together is a guarantee of successful interdisciplinary team work (Ovretveit, 1993). Organisational, professional and personal challenges similar to those encountered in developing interdisciplinary teamwork remain to be overcome (Barr, 1997). It is possible that the attraction of funding available for interdisciplinary research may result in a need to work closer together and in a paradoxical way lead to the development of the necessary motivation, knowledge, skills and understanding to facilitate interdisciplinary research.

Nurses and other professionals who engage in successful interdisciplinary research will need a broad knowledge base in relation to health and social care research methods. They also require skills in effective communication, including listening, questioning, assertiveness and negotiation. Above all they will need confidence in their abilities and the support of those close to them as they climb the steep learning curve often associated with interdisciplinary working and research. For their efforts professionals will gain new insights into health and social care and the contribution of colleagues.

It can be difficult when caught up in the practicalities of completing a project to clearly see the lessons that can be learnt from going through the process. It is therefore important to take time to reflect upon the lessons learnt in undertaking a research project such as a MSc, with a view to their implications for further studies. Once a project is completed temptation (grown out of being glad to have it finished) is not to look for the lessons to be learnt. All researchers, whether novice or experienced, should invest time in reflection once projects have been completed. From a personal perspective it is possible to identify several key lessons from undertaking the MSc that have a direct relevance to undertaking further studies in this area. In summary, these related to a period of time longer than anticipated to recruit adequate numbers of participants and the need to widen either inclusion criteria and/or time available in any further study. It also become clear that there was a need for increased collaboration with local services to understand the situations discussed by participants and reduce anxiety among local staff about the project. The need to manage time effectively was a key lesson learnt (gradually) as the time needed for reading, writing, interviews, data analysis and writing up became apparent. Through support from the research supervisor, important lessons were also learnt about the need to retain a focus on the project in hand and resist the temptation to stray off the main route and onto the 'side roads'. Indeed insights were gained into the process and aims of research supervision that confirm the process outlined earlier in the chapter. In hindsight, it would have been advantageous to clarify the nature and remit of supervision at the start of the project. Finally it is possible to learn a lot about oneself through completing a project. The need to plan well ahead, to restrict the amount of extra work taken on, to be realistic about personal resources and the need to retain a family life were all hard-earned personal insights. It was very beneficial to retain some recreational interest outside of the project – for me these were trips to the cinema and keeping up a commitment to fitness training. Although it was necessary to carefully plan in these activities, both of these interests provided a welcome break from the project thus helping to charge up personal batteries and maintain some form of sanity.

On a personal note, the investment required when undertaking a MSc that had an interdisciplinary aspect has been repaid in the insights and new knowledge gained, as well as the development of formal and informal networks that present new opportunities for further interdisciplinary research. Finally it was a tremendous opportunity (and privilege) to become sensitised to the pressure on parents' time and the competing demands they face in their daily lives.

ACKNOWLEDGEMENTS

To all parents and children who gave their time and energy during a difficult period for them so that I and others may understand more of how they perceive genetic counselling.

To staff at the Department of Medical Genetics at Belfast City Hospital for their assistance in accessing potential participants as well as their encouragement and interest in the project.

Importantly to Marie, our children and extended family and friends, as without their support this research and chapter would not have been completed.

SUPERVISOR'S COMMENTS
Robin Millar

Throughout this chapter references have been made to the potential functions of the research supervisor within the research process. At times it is the supervisor's subject knowledge or technical expertise that fulfils a need and helps the student researcher move forward. At other times it is more about being supportive, rewarding, challenging or simply bolstering sagging motivation and self-doubt. At any or all stages of the research process outlined earlier, potential threats exist which if shared can usually be overcome or their effects ameliorated. It is knowing what is required, when it is required and how to provide it that constitutes effective supervision.

Any research which attempts to span distinctive disciplines makes heavy demands on the supervisor. The need to be conversant with a familiar knowledge base may be insufficient when supporting interdisciplinary research. For example, the published knowledge within the medical field on, say, genetics or dealing with adult survivors of childhood abuse displays little connection to a related knowledge base to be found in the counselling and therapy literature. Of course a potential outcome of this perspective is to build bridges between hitherto unrelated literature – this makes considerable demands on the supervisor's specific expertise.

Similarly, different disciplines have very different traditions with respect to the research process. This places demands on supervisors to be conversant with a wide range of methodologies and is increasing both within and between disciplines. Indeed, earlier references to the pluralist approach serve to emphasise the importance of being aware of a full spectrum of research methods.

The significance of such awareness becomes important throughout the research process. Encouraging students and colleagues to think through the whole process from questions to design, analysis and discussion from the very beginning can be challenging. The desperate need to get started often requires the application of a 'handbrake', or the 'let's just think that through' type of question. I suspect we are often perceived as nuisances or 'spanners in the works' in the short term! However, the need to challenge thinking and opinions early may have important consequences in the longer term. Challenges to think ahead, to plan, to consider consequences of actions, to be sensitive to the needs of participants (whoever they might be) or to anticipate events and timescales may prove beneficial. Hopefully, a major outcome will be a clarity of thinking about the whole study *before* the start date or registration session.

Research students may also approach the research process with strong views about preferred methods, who to involve in the study and what type of analysis is to be carried out. Such views are often based on avoidance thinking and may be the result of very negative perspectives, such as 'I'm not using one of those computers', 'I'm no good with numbers', 'I want to do something where I can interview people', or 'I need to start tomorrow because I've got this group I can use'.

Moving towards the end of the process the interpretation of results can be driven by vested interests and the need to support certain outcomes (such as the efficacy of a particular intervention or educational programme). Where research is supported by organisations the possibility of conflicting agendas looms large and can introduce considerable difficulties for both researcher and supervisor. Such distortions or blind spots need to be challenged forcibly through the supervision process whatever philosophical approach has been adopted. In a number of ways the research process can be driven by the wrong determinants – the cart is often put before the horse!

Although difficult and unpopular, challenging such stances is a major function of the research supervisor because it is through these techniques that students develop a broader knowledge and understanding of the research process from beginning to end, in the correct order. Furthermore, students are required to extend the breadth of their knowledge as a basis for choice and action. They may need considerable encouragement to engage in reading around design and methodological considerations (in both texts and academic papers) as opposed to reading about the substantive content of the study – most are keen to do this. Indeed, frequently, supervisors need to curtail the extent of this latter type of reading in order to keep the study focus clear and circumscribed.

Finally, it is necessary to emphasise the more humanistic aspect of research supervision. Engaging in research, particularly interdisciplinary and/or field research, can be a frustrating and demoralising experience. The learning curve is often very steep indeed! Individual research students need support when progress seems absent, interest or enthusiasm expected from others is not forthcoming, participants are hard to find and then let you down just when you need them most and, after all these trials and tribulations, not one statistically significant result materialises… The feeling that it is the outcome of research that is most important may tempt students to write extensively about findings that fail to demonstrate statistical significance; that is, to over-report their results. Although understandable it is none the less unacceptable practice. Students need to realise that competence in carrying out each stage of the research process is what requires demonstration – the focus is on process rather than on product. However, 'good' results do wonders for motivation and the writing-up phase.

So, the research process is shared between researcher and supervisor. The researcher drives the car with the supervisor taking the passenger seat, both travelling on the same road with its hills and dales, its smooth and bumpy surfaces and the myriad of tempting side roads. The experience can be less like a casual Sunday outing and more like a car rally, with its peaks and troughs of emotion and with the supervisor working actively as part of the team, shouting out the pace notes to help the driver successfully negotiate the hazardous terrain. At times it may be tempting for the navigator/supervisor to seize the controls and assume the responsibility for driving the car. In general such actions should be resisted. Although victory itself may taste sweet, finishing the race may be equally rewarding for both driver and passenger.

REFERENCES

Ambler, S. (1997) Pharmacy practice – developing multidisciplinary research. *Journal of Interprofessional Care;* 11: 1, 67–75.

Barr, O. (1997) Interdisciplinary teamwork: consideration of the challenges. *British Journal of Nursing;* 6: 17, 1005–1110.

Bennett, B. (1998) Increasing collaboration within a multidisciplinary neurorehabilitation team: the early stages of a small action research project. *Journal of Clinical Nursing;* 3: 227–231.

Casey, A., Hoy, D. (1997) Language for research and practice. *Journal of Interprofessional Care;* 11: 1, 35–41.

Hennemann, E.A., Lee, J.L., Cohen, J. (1995) Collaboration: a concept analysis. *Journal of Advanced Nursing;* 21: 1, 103–109.

Lorentzon, M. (1995) Multidisciplinary collaboration: life lines or drowning pool for nurse researchers? (Guest editorial). *Journal of Advanced Nursing;* 22: 825–826.

Lorentzon, M. (1998) The way forward: nursing research or collaborative health care research? (guest editorial). *Journal of Advanced Nursing;* 27: 675–676.

Mackenzie, J., Husband, K., Gerrish, K. (1995) Researching in collaboration: a guide to successful partnership. *Nurse Researcher;* 3: 1, 83–89.

Marteau, T., Richards M. (1996) *The Troubled Helix: Social and Psychological Implications of the New Human Genetics.* Cambridge: Cambridge University Press.

Mason, T. (1997) Censorship of research in the health services setting. *Nurse Researcher*; 4: 4, 83–92.

Ovretveit, J. (1993) *Co-ordinating Community Care. Multidisciplinary Teams and Care Management.* Buckingham: Open University Press.

Parahoo, K. (1998) Research utilisation and research related activities of nurses in Northern Ireland. *Journal of International Nursing Studies*; 35: 283–291.

Polit, D.F., Hungler, B.P. (1997) *Nursing Research. Principles and Methods.* (6th edition). Philadelphia: JB Lippincott.

Rafferty, A.M., Traynor, M. (1997) On the state of play in nursing research. *Journal of Interprofessional Care*; 11: 1, 43–49.

Read, S. (1998) The context of nursing and health care research. (23–54). In: Crookes, P.A., Davies, S. (eds). *Research into Practice.* London: Baillière Tindall/RCN.

Rolfe, G. (1998) The theory-practice gap in nursing: from research-based practice to practitioner-based research. *Journal of Advanced Nursing*; 28: 3, 672–679.

Ross, F. (1996) Interprofessional audit: the need for teamwork when researching quality of care. *Nurse Researcher*; 3: 3, 47–57.

Ross, F., Meerabeau, L. (1997) Research and professional practice (editorial). *Journal of Interprofessional Care*; 11: 1, 5–7.

Seidman, I.E. (1991) *Interviewing as Qualitative Research. A Guide for Researchers in Education and the Social Sciences.* New York: Teachers College Press.

Thomas, P., Graver, L. (1997) The Liverpool intervention to promote teamwork in general practice: an action research approach. (174–191).In: Pearson, P. and Spencer, J. (eds). *Promoting Teamwork in Primary Care. A Research-based Approach.* London: Edward Arnold.

Wright, N., Furness, L., Molloy, C. (1997) A successful collaborative approach to the recruitment of patients with Alzheimer's disease to antidementia drug trials. *Journal of Interprofessional Care*; 11: 3, 325–333.

5. Research approaches: methodological tensions

Author
Dawn Hobson

Conmmentaries
Alfons Grieder
Julienne Meyer

INTRODUCTION

Receiving an invitation to undertake a piece of funded research of one's own choice, in order to register for a PhD, could be described as the research student's dream. It could also be recognised as a hangman's rope. The freedom to choose an area meant that I had the opportunity to combine two long-term interests, which were palliative care in the hospital environment and the use of applied academic philosophy in nursing. However, freedom also meant working in isolation, doubt and sometimes from little more than gut instinct. This chapter will detail the route from hazy ideas and idealistic visions to an actual research proposal. It will explore the instruments used to gather data and the tools used in analysis. It will also be a personal account of the experience of tackling the issues involved. The chapter concludes with comments from Dr Alfons Grieder, an academic philosopher who supervised the project, and further comments from Professor Julienne Meyer about the various benefits and detractions of selecting a supervisor external to nursing.

IDEALS AND VISIONS: BACKGROUND TO THE TOPIC

I am in the final stages of analysis and writing up of a PhD study which aims to identify and articulate the latent ethical dimension of nurses' work in caring for cancer patients in a hospital environment. To this end the project has involved one year's participant observation and 25 interviews with cancer nurses and associated doctors in a large cancer unit in a London teaching hospital. The research approach taken has drawn upon philosophical phenomenology, adapting data collection methods accordingly. This section outlines the development of ideas which has built, sometimes haphazardly, the study described.

Several years prior to the choosing of a topic, I had completed a small-scale research project for a BSc dissertation, which fostered an ongoing interest in palliative care (Powell, 1993). The study used qualitative methods to look at the effect on patient care of an explicit principle of including patients in treatment decisions. Using the example of a palliative care team within a London teaching hospital, patients were interviewed about their feelings and perceptions regarding their care. A series of complex issues emerged in relation to the provision of palliative care within a hospital environment.

These included patients' sense of anxiety and isolation in the process of dying. Related to this, nurses caring for the patients felt that there were blocks to the care they ideally wished to implement for patients. For instance, some nurses felt that patient care rested too much on medical science without due consideration of the associated ethical implications. These nurses also experienced difficulty in articulating the ethical implications and felt powerless to highlight their importance in multidisciplinary care planning. I became interested in the blocks which appeared to be getting in the way of nurses feeling better able to care for dying patients.

My interest in the use of philosophy in nursing arose from studying moral philosophy during nurse training and also while writing a masters degree dissertation on the status of moral knowledge (Hobson, 1995). I began to notice that there were links between the issues discussed particularly in applied moral philosophy, namely ethics and many patient care decisions involved on the wards where I had done the BSc project. The main link was the identification of underlying tensions in practice dilemmas. By isolating issues within practical events that related to ongoing philosophical discourses, it became clearer where the tensions in the situation actually lay. In extending the arguments a useful process of critical reflection began, furthering the debate in question and challenging assumptions. I became excited by the potential use of philosophy in giving a language to the difficult and uncomfortable aspects of palliative care I had observed in my BSc project.

I thus came to register for the PhD with clear interests and intentions. However, capitalising on previous experience and gut instinct does not mean going into the study knowing what will be found. It gives a flavour for what might be important, which needs to be supported by literature reviews, methodological advice and good supervision. In my case, this process caused a change of direction for the PhD.

REALITY: GETTING GOING

The areas I chose for my literature search were ethical theory, decision-making and clinical nursing practice. Two key strands emerged, which were taken to frame the research question. The first confirmed my earlier hunches that cancer nurses felt that their work generated moral questions which were difficult to articulate and address (Benoliel, 1993; Oberle, 1996). The second was the failure of theoretical ethical frameworks to meaningfully inform clinical practice (Elliott ,1993; Stoffell, 1994). This was the point where I had to change many of my ideas. These will be briefly examined in turn.

The first strand from the literature was the body of concern from cancer nurses that their work generated moral questions. This centred around the lack of a 'language' to articulate the issues involved. In turn, this was felt to impede interprofessional communication on some of the most important aspects of patient care. I noticed that few empirical studies addressing these concerns used data gathered from nurses actually in their clinical practice. Instead there was a predominance of hypothetical scenarios used to examine nurses' responses. Some research studies were beginning to point to the influence of contextual factors in ethical decision-making (Bergum, 1994; Sherblom, Shipps and Sherblom, 1993; Smith, 1996) and specifically to the role of the individual nurses' values and beliefs when encountering ethical difficulty (Oberle, 1996). There was also a move away from Kohlberg's traditional picture of moral development (Kohlberg, 1976). This had depicted justice rather than care as the most advanced form of moral reasoning. His research had again been conducted with hypothetical examples and was criticised for characterising care as inferior without understanding what it was. The result of these and other debates in the literature was repeated calls to pay more heed to the influence of the context in which nurses make ethical decisions. Despite this, very little research had taken place within a clinical area to investigate these matters further. Instead work had focused on developing ethical decision-making protocols, or philosophical training, or different 'ethical' policies. I felt that these were begging the question of what exactly the problems were in practice and whether there were distinctively ethical decisions.

The second strand from the literature was the problem with the implementation of moral 'frameworks' in practice. These frameworks, for example Kant's deontological approach, were used to guide decision-making by deducing right actions from a universal moral principle. Kant's universal moral principle is that actions can only be justified if the principle involved can have general applicability rather than just to the immediate situation (Korsgaard, 1989). For example, telling less than the truth to patients can never be seen to have universal acceptability. But it has been difficult for practitioners to deduce from general injunctions, like 'always tell the truth', what should actually be done in the 'nuts and bolts' of situations. It is not clear from this principle whether perhaps a slow disclosure of the truth to a frightened patient would be acceptable. The working definition of truth is not given in the framework. Even if it were, in order for it to be clinically relevant in different scenarios the definition would have to have endless caveats and justifications. This problem applies to frameworks in general (Dawson, 1994). There are competing available frameworks (such as Kant's) and the literature suggests that it has been difficult for practitioners to find any basis for choosing between them (Stoffell, 1994). I had not anticipated these difficulties. On further searching the literature it was possible to see that the theories concerned had largely been drawn from Anglo-American analytic philosophy, with characteristically abstract principles and rational individualism (Clarke and Simpson, 1989; Foot, 1979). There was a growing body of literature trying to redress these distortions, by looking at the non-rational parts of life and ideas of reciprocity and community. I became convinced that these approaches held more promise for the consideration of ethical issues in practice than those based on abstract principles, more commonly in use. This realisation had implications for my methodological approach, described later.

In summary, there were two central areas that were taken from the literature to frame the research question. These were, firstly, the difficulty in articulation that the nurses seemed to be experiencing. Within this was the unexamined role of values and beliefs and the need to properly take into account the situations in which ethical difficulties arose. Second was the rejection of abstract principles as a guide for practice, in favour of approaches more grounded in local practice and perception.

During the planning of the research I was attending seminars in other disciplines as well as nursing and trying to build up networks of contacts in my area of research. At a meeting of the London Medical Sociology group in 1997 I met with one key person who broadened my view of what the study could be and gave me further ideas for its implementation. This was Professor Renee Fox, who is an internationally known medical sociologist with particular expertise in the sociological aspects of bioethics. I thought how much I could benefit from her opinion of what I wanted to do. Despite fears about the underdeveloped nature of my ideas and relative inexperience in the field, I decided to ask for some time. I have found since that academics are often glad to share an interest about their subject and welcome debate. On this occasion, five hours of challenging discussion in the Senior Common Room of Balliol College Oxford resulted. This both reassured me and stimulated the development of my work in a way which has not lost impetus. Professor Fox felt that a philosophical study using classical field research methods would be interesting methodologically and well targeted for the specific area. She discussed with me fieldwork strategies, note-taking and analysis and warned me that I was not undertaking a psychological study of motivation and that there would be attendant cultural features. In going to presentations in my area of study and asking for help, I feel I received a generous and challenging contribution to my work. Discussing your research strategy with a person with 40 years of field work experience is much more influential than reading the texts – although this was also an essential part of my own development.

THE QUESTION(S) AND BEGINNINGS OF A METHOD

In choosing a method I needed the flexibility to explore individual perception as a basis for analysis and at the same time to witness those perceptions at work in the moral conflicts occurring in the clinical situation. I was not setting out to measure what the nurses said against what they actually did, but to see how they construed their work and the decisions that presented. This would be a way in to examining the situation as a whole, with consideration of environmental and cultural features.

Initially, all forms of qualitative social research were attractive. On closer reading, I found that several would not give the flexibility to explore individual perception as a basis for analysis. Methods drawing on symbolic interactionism and social realism (Strauss and Corbin, 1990; Miles and Huberman, 1994) relied on ideas of construction which I felt would not provide an adequate backdrop to the study of individual values and beliefs. Problems identified in the literature were starting with differences at this level, rather than being mainly defined by social boundaries. Guided by my supervisors, I began to examine the philosophical work of Heidegger, Dilthey and Jaspers, concentrating on Heidegger's main work, *Being and Time* (Heidegger, 1962). The clues I took from Heidegger's approach are centred around his analysis of how we understand and interpret ourselves in the world in which we find ourselves. The term 'being in the world' is a central concept representing the unity between ourselves and the 'world' (Solomon, 1972), in the sense that our world is constituted of things that show themselves up for us and have significance for us. In this way existential phenomenology is not merely concerned with interiority, but with people as 'situated' in the world. For Heidegger, existential meaning is to do with temporality: choosing possible ways-to-be in relation to the way one-has-been. The choosing of 'how to be' is unique to each person and raises the interesting notion of authentic and inauthentic voices. I was interested both in Heidegger's subject matter, that of existential meaning and significance and also his approach to analysing this. Broadly speaking, it is a hermeneutic exercise to interpret the meaning given to things. This is in contrast to methods isolating social relations without taking note of subjective concerns. Heidegger argues that it is by studying the involved practical viewpoint of people in situations that meaning and significance can be examined. He therefore insists that we return to the phenomenon of everyday human activity.

According to Heidegger, there is no such thing as an investigative process which takes nothing for granted. We must already have some understanding of something in order to question it. The turning round and studying the pretheoretical conditions of questioning is different from Husserl's transcendental meaning. Instead, in Heidegger's account, all comprehension relies on pre-conception and so interpretation is an essential business (Dreyfus, 1995). Finding in these concepts a powerful analysis and focus for researching perception, I began to look around for a methodological application.

PROBLEMS AND SOLUTIONS

Reading the work of researchers such as Tina Koch (Koch, Webb and Williams, 1995) and Peter Draper (1994) persuaded me that there were methodologies to be had from Heidegger's phenomenology of Being. I saw that they had used the methods to provide a platform for a richer analysis of multiple perspectives compared to other researchers in their field. The voices of participants were clearly apparent even in the final analysis and understanding was gained of these people's situations which was not merely descriptive. Having seen the benefits of the approach, I further examined the use of methods drawing on phenomenology in the nursing and psychotherapeutic research literature. I found that, like others (Cash, 1995; Paley, 1998), I was disappointed by the way in which many of the studies had, far from offering a more penetrating analysis than other methods, seemed to offer no analysis whatsoever. There were often exhaustive descriptions of particular experiences without any interpretive commentary or background context to give the reader a handle on the narrative extracts. However, rather than reject the method itself, I felt it was important to explore how the philosophy could be applied more usefully, as I had seen in the work of Koch et al (1995) and Kaufman (1988). I decided to begin by addressing the main criticisms of methods drawing on phenomenology, which were highlighting the weaknesses of published studies. The problems fell in the following categories, which will be described and discussed, followed by the solutions or adaptations I chose in order to use the approach:

▶ The nature of interpretation;

▶ The accusation of reading minds;

▶ What about culture, time and place?

The nature of interpretation

Despite its interpretive claims, methodologically it is unclear in many phenomenological studies how the process of interpretation is to be done. In the literature this seems to be part of a bigger problem, in that researchers have often assumed an uncomplicated leap from philosophical claims to research practice. Very often there was no clear link made between the two. Philosophical phenomenology gives clues as to an approach to being-in-the-world but the method it proposes is not empirical. The problem is to translate these clues into a research design that carries them forward. I found that instead, many articles claiming to draw on Heidegger described their philosophical basis and then immediately presented a version of textual analysis followed by the presentation of themes (Benner, 1994). This is no different from simplified forms of narrative analysis (Riessman, 1993). I found that there was often no account of the interpretation of meaning, as phenomenology would imply. There was also no account of how the philosophical nature of human *being* has influenced the process of data collection and analysis. I learnt that the term phenomenology was just a label in these studies and that the findings rarely gave anything other than descriptions of sense experience (personal communication: Grieder, 1997). There was little insight or genuine analysis to be gained from reading the reports. From the earlier work cited I could see that the approach had a genuine contribution to make, but the domination of poor application of philosophy to method in the research literature had given it a bad name.

I chose to approach this by using Heidegger's work as a series of clues rather than an entire philosophy which I had to somehow superimpose on the project. I could see nothing wrong with adapting known research tools to fit this purpose. I used the notion of interpretation to highlight the need for and inevitability of researcher involvement, to come to understand personally the situation and environment of the participants. I used the different elements of it to point to the various places where attention needs to be focused: on the participants' past experience and future aims, on how these shape their present perceptions and on how they relate to group structures. Interpretations can be erroneous and I checked them with participants on an ongoing basis for this reason (Clifford, 1983).

A second and related feature with which I was unhappy was the way that interpretive work in phenomenological analysis was often obscured by the detailing of validation measures. An example of this is the use of external auditors to verify that findings represent participants' experiences (Benner, 1994). However, if phenomenology is an interpreted account of understandings, an external authority cannot validate the subjective meaning attributed to events by participants. I chose to adopt forms of member-checking to address this more appropriately. I also spent a long period in the unit where the research took place to avoid making unwarranted and unsubstantiated judgements.

The problems with interpretation fed into a further critique of phenomenological methods in the literature known as descriptivism (Burrell and Morgan, 1979). This states that because the accounts of experience are inherently 'respectful' to participants, subsequent reports lack critical purchase. I suspect that the reason for the disappointing lack of analysis in the studies was a fear of distorting participants' views. As a result, nurse researchers can present sense experience as inviolable truth, reasoning that because participants are giving an interpreted account of their understanding, it cannot be subject to external critique (Benner, 1994). If a person said it, then that is all there is to say. I could see the tension between cross-case analysis and the need to preserve the 'face' of the individual at the same time (Hallett, 1998). I chose to deal with this by questioning whether the analysis had to be cross-case. Instead I analysed multiple perspectives for types of experiences which were first developed at the individual level. In the analysis I also used field notes from participant observation to ensure that relevant features of the research setting were used as context. I found that this was a vital means of 'fleshing out' the meaning of colloquial terms and gaining understanding of participants' work situation. I also used known aspects of the research process, such as the difference between public and private accounts (Cornwell, 1984), in order to design and carry out the interviewing and observation. I did not feel that this would jeopardise the individual contribution. I felt that I had to develop a critical analysis, given my access to multiple perspectives and the social environment. This interpretive effort was then given back to individual participants and others in similar settings for validation purposes. In the end, interpretive research would be self-defeating if the end product were not a synthesis of both the researcher's interpreted analysis and participants' feedback. This is because philosophical concepts about the way we experience the world around us apply as much to researchers as to those taking part in the research.

The accusation of reading minds

The second strand of criticism was a concern with the aim of phenomenology, both as a philosophy and as a base for qualitative research, of laying out the nature of a person's world – that is, how they have understood it. The criticism is that, if the researcher always comes across things because of interpreted significance, as Heidegger puts it, they cannot then claim to lay out the nature of another's 'world' and how they construe it. Schwandt (1994) replies to this problem by turning the question on its head, asking if there is any qualitative research that does not in fact rest on an interpreted account of the participants' understanding. There can be no unmediated access to views and opinions, experiences and values, nor can they be excluded from responses. In that sense, I could only write with authority of my own opinions, experience and values. I concluded that the end product can only be an approximation. Within that I took several things into account. Using participant observation meant that the interpretation was not only based on verbal expression, which has been highlighted by various authors as a difficulty when working with nurses who feel disempowered and unseen (Reed, 1994). I saw that interviews alone would not necessarily give privileged access to nurses' experience. The over-reliance on the open-ended interview in qualitative research has been criticised elsewhere (Atkinson and Silverman, 1997).

I explored ways of complementing this approach, such as entering the nurses' clinical situation and becoming part of it. I used this as another means of establishing a participants' world-view and having a sufficiently individualised context in order to do so (Burgess, 1989). It also meant that multiple methods of data collection were employed and links between them were formed in the analysis (Fielding and Fielding, 1986). In this way a broader account of participants' understandings was achieved. Having acknowledged that as a researcher I was far from being a blank slate for others' experiences, I found that having a nursing background was useful in developing trust and acceptance among the staff of the unit. This was because I could understand how to participate and help, made easier by wearing uniform. I could identify with the work they were doing and the issues being faced, having been in similar situations myself. Access to the participants was therefore made easier by trust and a strong sense of identification. This has been documented as a positive feature in other research studies undertaken by nurses in hospitals (Savage, 1995). The problems with over-familiarity and how to deal with them are also well documented (Kleinman and Copp, 1993). I found that over time it was difficult to keep a critical distance from situations on the ward. I dealt with this mainly by having clinical supervision, which is described later.

What about culture, time and place?

The third strand of criticism was the concern over the way in which time, place and culture are not paid due attention in phenomenology, given the emphasis on the life-world (Latimer, 1998). I did not find this as problematic as the first two, because I thought it must be possible to retain the individual contribution without ignoring the entire social situation in which people live and work. I found that looking at culture, time and place was essential in order to lay out the influences perceived by the individual nurse and to examine how they established themselves in the 'everyday', or 'the they' as Heidegger puts it. However, the approach was different in focus to a study of social practices. I looked from the individual perspective out and this is simply a complement to other approaches. In order to bring sociocultural issues to the analysis I concentrated particularly on the links between the field notes and interviews. Ways of dealing with death and dying in an acute context featured strongly in this.

ADAPTATION

Having chosen a phenomenological approach to understanding, state of mind and language and aware of the sometimes fierce criticisms of this method, I gathered a series of tools with which to proceed. These were, broadly speaking, participant observation, semi-structured interviewing with cancer nurses and associated doctors, and the tracking of patients whose care was identified to involve an ethical concern. Participant observation included a form of 'moral witnessing' as Professor Fox has termed it.. This involved noting resistances, impasses and problems relating to ethical concerns, such as the degree to which people can and do talk about them. It involved observing what happened when the issues were raised and what is conceived as ethical. It allowed me to observe critical incidents from an inside view of the world of nurses.

Through a series of ward visits to explain the research and subsequent ethics committee approval, I negotiated a participant-observer research role on an oncology unit. I participated in the provision of care to 20 cancer patients, wearing uniform and having an honorary contract with the ward in order to do so. The aim of this was to literally share in the nurses' practice and everyday concerns, to gain background for their perspectives. I found that the nurses and doctors on the unit were welcoming and open, identifying that the issues I had come to study were pertinent and challenging. The difficulties and dilemmas of researching this area were nonetheless often increased by understandable defence strategies, which eased with time in the unit. Throughout this period I was aware of a sense of having touched a 'raw nerve' and interestingly this never eased.

I worked alongside an individual nurse each shift, to witness the practices involved, come to interpret his or her understanding of situations as they arose and also record what I perceived them to be. Field notes were taken for 12 months, recording each day the conversations, events and interpretations I shared in. I used Labov's approach to structuring personal narratives for this, which have the aim of constructing a story from primary experience and interpreting the significance of events in embedded evaluation (Labov, 1972). He argues that narratives have formal structures which include an abstract or summary of the narrative, an orientation giving details of the situation and participants, the sequence of events, an evaluation of the significance and meaning of the action, a resolution and a coda, which returned the perspective to the present, specifying implications for how to proceed with the research. I found that structuring my observations in this way helped me to 'process' the day, to work out what I had interpreted from what and to give a rationale for selective recording.

Interviews took place between periods of shadowing and were informal dialogues where nurses were asked to talk further and explore areas of concern in their field of practice. Many texts on interviewing suggest that meaning is jointly constructed between interviewer and respondent (Mishler, 1991) and this came to have more and more pertinence for me. I found that unstructured interviews in the area of ethics, where language is such a problem anyway, were not empowering nurses to express their experiences. I found instead that questions and responses were developed and shaped by dialogue between us. I don't mean that I was sharing my experiences but that by listening to the answers to questions it was possible to see their interpretation of the question and to let this shade the meaning constructed. Questions became part of a circular process in this way. By recording details such as pauses and emphasis it is possible for this process and the developing meaning to become clearer. After the interview I would return to working alongside the nurses. Thus a broader understanding could be gained and there was more opportunity for nurses to continue to speak about issues they had often considered openly for the first time in the interview.

Hermeneutic analysis, which was originally a method of studying biblical texts, was used to analyse the transcripts and field notes. Riessman (1993) argues that analysis is not easily distinguished from transcription and that arranging and rearranging texts in the light of our discoveries tests, clarifies and deepens our understanding of what is happening. Analysis involves asking questions of the data, such as how is it organised; why is it developed in this way; starting from meanings encoded in the text and bringing to the interpretation the social, cultural and institutional discourses in which they are situated (Riessman, 1993). I will be using Heidegger's exploration of the nature of experience to generate exemplars. I have taken this from Benner to mean narrative examples of experiences which have 'family resemblances' to similar embodied experiences. In this way the data can be represented in a manageable size but still describe the phenomenon with the background needed. Findings will outline the tension that I have seen between the individual and the institution and between breaking out of, or being constrained by, inarticulate unease about situations that are perceived to involve compromised patient care.

There is a positivist tension in doing this kind of work which is shown for me in wanting to come out of the study with a few neat conclusions that can be separated out and presented. One's own interests and understandings are part of the process in this work and are unavoidable. The need to get alongside participants and engage in their environment is not only taxing but likely to affect the nurses' perception of ethical issues and their handling of them. It is possible to document these changes so they can become part of the data collected. In my study the nurses said to me after a few months they had got so used to me that they were fed up with being on guard and would rather I saw it as it was for them anyway – although there was still greater awareness shown by looking at me whenever the word 'ethical' was mentioned.

KEEPING GOING

Given the difficulties encountered in undertaking a PhD, it is essential to maintain one's motivation. For me, my motivation was a desire to improve patients' isolation whilst dying in hospital. My previous personal experience of cancer nursing had convinced me, I suspect unlike any literature review could, of the importance of the unseen blocks to providing effective palliative care in an acute environment. Knowing that there is something to be found, without knowing what it is and how it is shaped, gave the study drive and endurance. However, one of the biggest struggles was with self-doubt, especially at the point of member-checking. I had some difficult issues to feed back, namely that for many different reasons, perceptions of ethical problems were impeding active management of the issues. I saw the responsibility of the trust given to me by the nurses and doctors in the study and I wondered if I had betrayed their friendship and honesty – which had been hard won. At these times it was crucial to have support from supervisors but, in addition, from a person not connected with the research. For me, the person knew the issues likely to be involved and provided clinical supervision for the time I was on the unit and analysing the data. This was a source of sanity and an essential forum in which to examine the boundaries of involvement and responsibility which were so blurred at times.

Having an existential philosopher as a co-supervisor continually provided a sense of direction during the methodological choices I faced. During the data collection we did feel as if we were on other sides of the world, but communication across them made me address the issue of how exactly the philosophy was informing what I was doing. Later, in the analysis, some of the findings were usefully supported with other areas of existential philosophy, challenging my understanding and deepening the whole effort. Applying existential philosophy to underpin nursing practice can seem a complex enterprise, especially as it is possible to become so part of the everyday ward life that a coherent research role is difficult to sustain. This approach openly acknowledges the role of interpretation in all human science and enables you to set out precisely the nature of what you have done. The best part of all is that I feel it has allowed me to stay as true to the phenomenon under study as it is possible to get.

ACKNOWLEDGEMENTS

I am very grateful to my supervisors, Dianne Yarwood, Head of Behavioural and Biological Sciences at St Bartholomew School of Nursing and Midwifery, City University and Dr Alfons Grieder, then Reader in Philosophy at City University. I am also thankful for the clinical supervision provided by Dr Angela Cotter, Senior Research Fellow, St Bartholomew School of Nursing and Midwifery, City University. The scholarship enabling me to do the research was provided by the Joint Research Board of St Bartholomew's Hospital and I am very grateful for their support. Thanks are also due to Dr Julienne Meyer, Reader in Adult Nursing at City University, for patient reviewing of drafts of this chapter.

SUPERVISOR'S COMMENTS
Dr Alfons Grieder

It may seem strange at first that a philosopher-phenomenologist should be involved in the supervision of a PhD thesis in nursing studies. It is well known, however, that whenever a science takes a new direction and is groping for a novel 'paradigm', then philosophy may be able to make its contribution by articulating the new field of research in a preliminary manner and by suggesting an appropriate methodology. Dawn's project indicates that nursing studies may, in some areas, have arrived at such a juncture. She was well advised to look over the fence; for where pioneering thought is taking shape, philosophy is never far away and usually part of the 'game', in one way or another.

Phenomenology is sometimes viewed as a purely philosophical matter, an approach which concerns philosophers only. It is true that the so-called phenomenological movement was primarily a philosophical enterprise and one of the more original philosophical developments to emerge in the 20th century. However, its significance extends far beyond philosophy; in particular, it has been a great inspiration in the field of human studies as well as in border areas between the human and natural sciences (for example, in psychology, psychiatry and psychotherapy). It is of importance wherever researchers are interested in, and come to terms with, what we may call the phenomena of subjectivity, that is consciousness and the way humans understand or experience themselves, others and the world around them.

The phenomenological movement was to some extent a reaction against certain prevailing naturalistic, objectivistic and positivistic trends in the human studies, a tendency to be 'more scientific' by putting the emphasis on the outwardly observable and measurable. It was a protest in the name of the subject, a protest against the attempt to marginalise subjectivity, that is the phenomena of consciousness and of existential comportment.

Given Dawn's main objective, her inquiry into nursing practice in a cancer ward would have been highly incomplete and hardly very informative had she not made this concerted effort to come to terms with a whole range of 'subjective' phenomena, such as how the nurses perceive their role and situation in the ward, the choices they face and how they make their decisions, as well as their personal ethical and world-views. Such phenomena are not outwardly observable and hardly quantifiable. A framework is required to articulate them and make us aware of the basic structure of human existential comportment.

A number of difficult methodological problems arise and Dawn has bravely grasped the nettles. Existential phenomenology was the work of philosophers with their specific philosophical interests. It is concerned with the general structures of existential comportment, that is structures which characterise human existence as such; among them the Heideggarian existential of Understanding, which seems particularly relevant for Dawn's work. However, an empirical inquiry such as the one she pursues is in the end not so much concerned with Understanding as such, but with this or that individual's existential understanding. Indeed, philosophical phenomenology can and should inform all research of this kind, although it cannot provide a sufficient basis for it. As Dawn has rightly seen, the general phenomenological directives have to be complemented by both hermeneutic interpretation and participant observation. She had to adopt a multi-dimensional approach, with phenomenology as one essential component. Let those who raise their critical (and sometimes badly prejudiced) objections show us how they can do better!

Dawn's project has involved the application of one discipline to another, which involves a different set of skills to those involved in purely philosophical study. She has had to develop philosophical concepts further than their original meaning to help explain the discoveries she has made. Supervision has therefore been work for both of us, in taking phenomenology to underpin accounts of nursing experience and looking for new ways to highlight the depth of nurses' work.

SUPERVISOR'S COMMENTS
Julienne Meyer

It is clear from Dawn's and Alfons' account that her PhD in nursing is pioneering a new field of research. The value of selecting a supervisor external to nursing, in this case a philosopher-phenomenologist, allows the researcher greater opportunity to extend the boundaries of previous thought in nursing. However, this should not underplay the unique value of being a nurse researcher nor the importance of remaining in close contact with one's own discipline.

Dawn's work not only adds to the body of knowledge on ethical decision-making in nursing, but also extends methodological understanding. By adopting a multi-dimensional approach, with phenomonology as one essential component, she makes a special contribution to research both within and outside her discipline.

Working across disciplinary boundaries can be both exciting and daunting. Dawn has drawn on her own personal strengths and experience in choosing her research question and data collection techniques, but she has also braved a 'new world' by challenging her own assumptions and engaging in wider academic debate. She has not chosen to replicate previous work but build her own approach and the results are inspiring.

Other PhD students following her advice should note the importance of self-motivation, intellectual curiosity and the need for support outside of academic supervision. There is increasing recognition of the impact on the researcher of doing sensitive research (Renzetti and Lee, 1993). Much of what concerns nurses brings them into sensitive areas and Dawn has chosen a particularly challenging area in which to work. In addition she has chosen to foster links across disciplines, synthesising perspectives and generating new ideas. This requires particular interpersonal skills which nurses often enjoy. While frequently dogged by self-doubt and uncertainty due to their socialisation in hierarchical contexts, nurses should remember their own special skills. It is evident that Dawn was able to work very closely with staff on an oncology unit and explore their world. It could be argued that her skills in being a nurse gave her privileged access to do so. As a result the findings of the research are likely to be more meaningful and of greater value to health care practitioners. By choosing an external supervisor but remaining true to nursing she has demonstrated the true value of interprofessional research.

REFERENCES AND BIBLIOGRAPHY

Atkinson, P., Silverman D. (1997) Kundera's immortality: the interview society and the invention of the self. *Qualitative Inquiry;* 3: 3, 304–325.

Barrett, S.R. (1996) *Anthropology: A Student's Guide to Theory and Method.* Toronto: University of Toronto Press.

Benner, P.E. (1994) *Interpretive Phenomenology.* London: Sage Publications

Benoliel, J.Q. (1993) The moral context of oncology nursing. *Oncology Nursing Forum Supplement;* 20: 10, 5–11.

Bergum, V. (1994) Knowledge for ethical care. *Nursing Ethics;* 1: 2, 71–79.

Burgess, R.G. (1989) Approaches to field research. In: Burgess, R.G (ed.) (1989) *Field Research: A Sourcebook and Field Manual.* London and New York: Routledge.

Burrell, G., Morgan, G. (1979) *Sociological Paradigms and Organizational Analysis.* London: Heinemann.

Cash, K. (1995) Benner and expertise in nursing: a critique. *International Journal of Nursing Studies;* 32: 6, 527–534.

Clarke, S.G., Simpson E. (1989) *Anti-theory in Ethics and Moral Conservatism.* New York: State University of New York Press.

Clifford, J. (1983) On ethnographic authority. *Representations;* 1: 118–146.

Cornwell, J. (1984) *Hard-Earned Lives: Accounts of Health and Illness from East London.* London and New York: Tavistock Publications.

Dawson, A.J. (1994) Professional codes of practice and ethical conduct. *Journal of Applied Philosophy;* 11: 2, 145–153.

Draper, P. (1994) *Promoting the Quality of Life of Elderly People in Nursing Home Care: A Hermeneutical Approach.* Unpublished PhD thesis, Hull.

Dreyfus, H.L. (1995) *Being-in-the-World.* Massachusetts: MIT Press.

Elliott, C. (1993) Where ethics comes from and what to do about it. *Hastings Centre Report;* 22: 4, 28–35.

Fielding, N.G., Fielding, J.L. (1986) Linking data. In: Van Maanen, J., Manning, P.K., Miller, M.L. (eds) *Qualitative Research Methods.* Newbury Park, London: Sage Publications.

Foot, P. (1979) *Theories of Ethics.* Oxford Readings in Philosophy. Oxford: Oxford University Press.

Hallett, C. (1998) The general and the particular in phenomenological research. In: *The Leading Edge, International Nursing Research Conference.* Edinburgh.

Heidegger, M. (1962) *Being and Time*. Translated by MacQuarrie and Robinson. New York: Harper and Row.

Hobson, D. (1995) *The Status of Moral Knowledge: Possibility and Structures*. Unpublished Master of Letters dissertation, St Andrews University, Scotland.

Holmes, C. (1996) The politics of phenomenological concepts in nursing. *Journal of Advanced Nursing*; 24: 579–587.

Kaufman, S.R. (1988) Toward a phenomenology of boundaries. *Medical Anthropology Quarterly*; 2: 8, 338–354.

Kleinman, S., Copp, M.A. (1993) *Emotions and Fieldwork*. London: Sage Publications.

Koch, T., Webb, W., Williams, A. (1995) Listening to the voices of older patients: an existential-phenomenological approach to quality assurance. *Journal of Clinical Nursing*; 4: 185–193.

Kohlberg, L. (1976) Moral stages and moralization: the cognitive-developmental approach. In: Lickona, T. (ed.) *Moral Development and Behavior: Theory, Research and Social Issues*. New York: Holt, Rinehart & Winston.

Korsgaard, C. (1989) Kant's analysis of obligation: the argument of foundations I. *Monist*; 72: 311–40.

Labov, W. (1972) The transformation of experience in narrative syntax. In: Labov, W. (ed.) *Language in the Inner City: Studies in the Black English Vernacular*. Philadelphia: University of Pennsylvania Press.

Latimer, J. (1998) Commonalities were found in meanings, situations and life experiences of women who survived breast cancer: commentary. *Evidence-Based Nursing*; 1: 1, 31.

Miles, M.B., Huberman, A.M. (1994) *Qualitative Data Analysis*. London: Thousand Oaks, London, New Delhi: Sage Publications.

Mishler, E.G. (1991) *Research Interviewing: Context and Narrative*. Massachusetts and London: Harvard University Press.

Oberle, K. (1996) Measuring nurses' moral reasoning. *Nursing Ethics*; 2: 4, 303–313.

Paley, J. (1998) Misinterpretive phenomenology. *Journal of Advanced Nursing*; 27: 817–824.

Powell, D. (1993) *An Exploration into Palliative Care in a Hospital Environment*. Unpublished BSc dissertation. London: City University.

Reed, J. (1994) Phenomenology without phenomena: a discussion of the use of phenomenology to examine expertise in long-term care of elderly patients. *Journal of Advanced Nursing*; 19: 336–341.

Renzetti, C.M., Lee, R.M. (1993) *Researching Sensitive Topics*. London: Sage Publications.

Riessman, C.K. (1993) *Narrative Analysis*. Edited by Manning, P.K. , Van Maanen, J., Miller, M.L. Qualitative Research Methods Series 30. London:Thousand Oaks, New Delhi: Sage Publications.

Savage, J. (1995) *Nursing Intimacy*. Harrow: Scutari.

Schwandt, T.A. (1994) *Constructivist, Interpretivist Approaches to Human Inquiry*. Edited by Denzin, N.K., Lincoln, Y.S. *Handbook of Qualitative Research*. London: Thousand Oaks, New Delhi: Sage Publications.

Sherblom, S., Shipps, T.B., Sherblom, J.C. (1993) Justice, care and integrated concerns in the ethical decision making of nurses. *Qualitative Health Research*; 3: 4, 442–464.

Smith, K.V. (1996) Ethical decision-making by staff nurses. *Nursing Ethics;* 3: 1, 17–25.

Solomon, R.C. (1972) *From Rationalism to Existentialism*. Lanham, New York: University Press of America.

Stoffell, B. (1994) Ethical praxis analysing ethics. *Health Care Analysis*; 2: 4, 306–309.

Strauss, A.L., Corbin, J. (1990) *Basics of Qualitative Research: Grounded Theory Procedures and Techniques*. Newbury Park, CA: Sage Publications.

6. Selecting a subject: problems and solutions

Author
Bill Stein

Commentaries
Professor John Reid
Professor Jennifer Hunt

INTRODUCTION

At the time of writing this chapter I am in the process of studying, on a part-time basis, for a PhD at Glasgow Caledonian University where I am also a lecturer. Initially, I registered for an MPhil with the possibility of transfer to PhD. Having completed three years of part-time study I have now satisfied the requirements of the university to allow me to transfer to PhD registration and I plan to submit my thesis after a further two years of study.

The working title of my thesis is 'The use of standardised scales and measures for identification, assessment and control of risk in mental health'. My background in 'risk' is in insurance. I have over 20 years of commercial insurance practice behind me and, in addition to a first degree in business and administration, I have obtained, by examination, the Fellowship qualification of the Chartered Insurance Institute. I joined Glasgow Caledonian University over six years ago to teach 'risk and financial services' and have become increasingly involved in the broader field of 'risk management' of which insurance forms only a part.

WHY A RESEARCH DEGREE?

I did not *have* to undertake a research degree as a condition of my employment, but it seemed clear to me that the best way to learn how to research would be to take this course. It also seemed the most appropriate way for a late entrant to the academic world (bringing business experience rather than a string of publications) to gain acceptance by 'career' academics.

It has been said that a research degree is as much about *learning to research* as it is about exploring a particular subject. I find that as I progress I am able to agree with that more and more. Also, I find that learning by the example of others is really the only effective approach. Careful reading of published research is of course one way, but taking every opportunity to attend the presentation of papers and to participate in the subsequent question-and-answer sessions also helps. This interest in the work of others changes over time. It seems to shift from initially only being attracted by the topic, style and layout of research papers towards *how* the researchers achieved what they set out to do and to consider flaws in their arguments or methods.

SELECTING A SUBJECT

It may help the reader to understand my particular search for a topic if I begin with a brief explanation of the term 'risk management'. There is an established body of literature about the principles of risk management. In all fields of endeavour risks have always been assessed – even if only intuitively. However, an organised risk assessment procedure has become more widespread with the development of risk management in industry and commerce since the 1950s. More recently, risk assessment procedures have been adopted by social services and psychologists, for example in child care cases where there may be a risk of abuse and in health care generally (Roberts and Holly, 1996). There is a growing literature about its clinical application in psychiatry (Carson, 1991; Monaghan, 1993; Carson, 1994; Grounds, 1995; Moore, 1995; Potts, 1995; Vinestock, 1996). At the core of a structured approach to risk management is a simple, repeatable cycle of activity: risk identification (what risks? – what sets of circumstances?); risk assessment or analysis (how much, how often? – prioritising for action); and risk control or transfer (physical controls, procedural controls, use of contract terms or by insurance). It would have been perfectly normal, and indeed compatible with my teaching, to have selected an insurance topic as my subject. However, I saw the health care field as an opportunity to develop some in-depth knowledge of risk management in an area where insurance-based solutions to risks were not the norm and where all effort had to go into risk reduction and control.

It seems to me that there are two possible outcomes which may arise from choosing a topic about which one does not already possess an in-depth knowledge. On the one hand, the end product may be superficial, with obvious omissions (obvious to subject experts, that is) and not of much value to professionals working in that field. On the other hand, provided that the basic subject homework is done and obvious gaffes avoided, it is possible that as an informed onlooker one can often see things not obvious to those working at close quarters. A visiting researcher may also be willingly regarded as a 'free' test, or audit, of the robustness of a system even when it is generally regarded by participants as working well. Seeking to apply knowledge from one field to new areas may also help in the search for some new *contribution to knowledge*. Initially it is difficult to accept that it is not necessary to discover some 'earth-shattering' new idea or fact and that some smaller more mundane contribution may suffice. Many ideas have already been tackled or have work in progress in some way, though finding out about that may be difficult. A mix of disciplines may make it more likely that some unique approach can be developed – and that it will remain unique throughout the life of the degree project. After all, a lot can happen in one or two years, but with part-time degrees taking perhaps up to six years to complete, it is important to minimise the chance of the work being overtaken by others.

Although television programmes frequently hold health workers up as heroes, the media, particularly the tabloid newspapers, treat them harshly when things go wrong. The mistakes of individual doctors, or of entire hospital departments, are given prominent treatment. There is much anecdotal evidence but only a limited number of authoritative studies on clinical risk or non-clinical risk (National Audit Office, 1996; Walshe and Dineen, 1998). All evidence points to high and rising costs of risk. I reasoned that any contribution to practice which ultimately helps to lower (or at least to slow the rate of increase in) the cost of risk must surely be beneficial.

Health providers face many risks ranging through failure to safeguard their patients, the fabric and equipment of the hospital, their staff, to protection of the environment and the general public. Mistakes by surgeons, obstetricians and midwifes and by cancer screening services are amongthose resulting in huge payouts. Mental health has some particularly difficult risk management areas in risks like patient suicide or homicide. Such risks are *low* in frequency but, when they happen, are *high* in severity. It was also suggested to me that mental health is something of a 'Cinderella' subject and less well researched than other medical specialisms – the inference being that mental health professionals might more readily take an interest in my research.

BACK TO BASICS – NHS RESEARCH TRAINING

I understand that most research degree programmes will incorporate some element of research training. I was fortunate to have some freedom to choose the training which seemed most appropriate to my specific needs. I attended a research methods training course and a separate three day health service research methods course, both at Glasgow University. The experience was an invaluable confidence builder and stimulated many new ideas. I found it particularly helpful to join in with the nurses and doctors attending the health service course as it helped me to make contacts and learn more about the culture of the health service and how it operates. As an outsider I do experience difficulty in gaining a clear understanding of how the health service works. The NHS is awash with codes and acronyms for job grades, titles, departments, specialisms, ailments, treatments and procedures which cannot be picked up from a single textbook. It is a gradual process of assimilation. Visits to hospitals and conversations with health workers from a variety of backgrounds, seniorities and geographical locations, all help to piece together a view of this highly complex organisation. I take every opportunity to attend conferences relative to health research and have attended an international symposium on mental health nursing, the annual conference of MIND (the mental health charity) and the annual conferences of the Nursing Research Initiative for Scotland. This helped to keep me in touch with active research practitioners as well as academics. All provide networking opportunities, of course, but I find that paying attention to the papers and to the speakers provides the best return on the time expended. A word of caution – offers of help enthusiastically given by conference delegates during coffee breaks frequently fail to materialise afterwards. However, a direct approach to a speaker (at the time, or by letter afterwards) has proved to be helpful on more than one occasion. Most speakers are likely to appreciate interest and to respond to a request for some specific piece of information or reference, rather than to some general appeal for help.

To obtain a greater appreciation of the diversity of current practice I visited four mental health trusts (two in Scotland and two in England) and carried out interviews with four different consultant psychiatrists. In addition I made two separate visits to the State Hospital at Carstairs – one to discuss risk assessment and later to hear a presentation on a computerised risk assessment tool being developed at Broadmoor Special Hospital. I received information and support from the Mental Welfare Commission for Scotland and met with a Mental Health Adviser from the Scottish Health Advisory Service. I also attended a full day training course for clinicians in the use of a risk assessment tool currently under trial in the south of England.

WHERE TO BEGIN – REVIEW OF LITERATURE AND PRACTICE

Before spending time on a literature search I found it helpful to browse through some of the many research methods texts just to consider conceptual issues, for example making the distinction between positivistic methodologies and phenomenological methodologies (Denscome, 1998; Holloway, 1997; Hussey, 1997; Phillips and Pugh, 1987; Blaxter, et al, 1996; Cormack, 1996; Holloway and Wheeler, 1996; Bell, 1993.) It helps immensely to be able to check out your understanding of these different research paradigms with more experienced researchers. Much better to risk embarrassing ignorance at this stage than much later on.

Searching literature and investigating practice is akin to a major piece of detective work. It is best to follow up all leads but to assume that some lines of enquiry will draw a blank. Much of my initial work was concerned with generating or refining my research topic. Once the topic was settled upon, the work of reviewing literature became a specific stage in my investigation of the chosen area. Be prepared to change and adapt as time passes and as your knowledge of the topic grows – this applies both to selecting a subject and a methodology. Plans which initially seem feasible may seem much less convincing after a few months of literature review and of discussion with the experts in the field.

Most novice researchers will have experience of searching and reviewing literature at Honours degree level or at Masters level. However, this process is raised to a higher level for a research-based degree. For one thing, the volume of literature is likely to be much greater. For another, the range of routes to discover relevant items is likely to be much more diverse. Having learnt by my mistakes I would recommend that every effort is made to engage the help of a university librarian when constructing multi-stage searches. After much effort on my own I did eventually turn to our faculty librarian to trawl the computerised databases in medicine, nursing, psychiatry and psychology – the results of the various searches demonstrated to me how much skill is needed to conduct them effectively. I also sought advice on relevant literature from speakers at the conferences I attended. I reviewed over 200 refereed journal articles, books and government publications by over 100 authors writing in the area of risk and mental health, mostly published between 1990 and 1998. There are plenty of book chapters on the subject of literature reviews but I recommend finding and reading an assortment of published literature reviews. You will soon be able to form a judgement that one is better than another and you will be able to hold this model in your mind.

I found it essential to be very methodical. I ensured that I stored all my reference material in such a way that I could find my way back to any item. I did not waste time reading papers without making some notes at the same time. As a researcher you will read so much that it will be impossible to retain key points unless they are written down. I considered at the outset the use of bibliographic software such as *Endnotes*. This is very much a matter of personal preference and simple note cards, used well, may be much better than computer software used badly. However, the main point is to sort this out at the beginning because it will be an unnecessary irritation to have to change methods mid-investigation.

There is a distinction to be made between background reading and a proper review; while speed reading will help to sort out papers into some rough hierarchy of relevance, thereafter there is no substitute for slow, careful reading, reflecting and putting thoughts down in print.

I have found it invaluable to take every opportunity to present my ideas to my peers. From a relaxed presentation to fellow research methods students, to a formal paper at a conference, any such public airing of ideas will force a reassessment of progress and help to review and restate one's ideas and methods. In addition, I have found you are more than likely to get some friendly help from the audience. In my own case I made several presentations to research group meetings within the university. I also presented a paper, based upon my review of literature and practice, at an international symposium on health and risk.

PRELIMINARY LITERATURE REVIEW FINDINGS

Most mental health patients are now managed in open wards or in the community. Although this provides a more normal life-style than that of locked wards in large hospitals for the majority of those with mental disorder, there is a small but significant risk of violence from a minority of patients. References to discharge and continuing community care emphasise the involvement of a large group of people, from patient to family carers, social workers, community mental health nurses, the patient's general practitioner and other community, residential and day care staff (NHS Management Executive, 1994). Before discharge there must be a careful assessment by both the multidisciplinary team responsible for a patient in hospital and those who will be taking the responsibility for his or her care in the community (NHS Management Executive, 1994).

The search for information looks at the past, the present and the future. Relevant factors include family background; attitudes of and to parents and siblings; history of physical or emotional abuse; history of mental disorder, suicide alcohol or drug use, criminality or violence; early relationships with peers, for example, bullying or being a victim of bullying; work history; reasons for ending particular work and problems with routine or authority. The list goes on and on.

Looking forward in time, the aim is to anticipate potential repetition of context and so to specify how and in what circumstances harm may occur; what may make it more or less likely; what the nature of the harm may be; how soon such a situation may develop; and for how long such a risk may be likely to persist (Grounds, 1995; Vinestock, 1996). Relevant factors are: family support; significant other support; employment; accommodation; finances; likely situations and relationships, including possible problems and possible victims.

Reed (1997) observes that the risks are summative, so that a person with a psychopathic disorder *and* an active psychotic illness who also misuses drugs and/or alcohol may present a very significantly increased risk to others. The best predictors of future offending among mentally disordered people are the same as those for the rest of the population – previous offending, criminality in the family, poor parenting and so on. Accurate information about past behaviour is particularly important since the best predictor of violence is past violence (Scott, 1997; Reed, 1997). As the Kim Kirkman inquiry reported: 'Nothing predicts behaviour like behaviour' (West Midlands Regional Health Authority, 1991).

The most commonly used measure of violent behaviour is conviction for a violent offence. But clearly many acts of violence never result in conviction. Other possibilities are, for example, arrest rates, or self-reported anti-social behaviour (Lipsedge, 1995). Most studies concentrate on variables that can be obtained easily and these variables tend to relate to sociodemographic status and criminal record. In other words there is an understandable tendency to measure the easily measurable. This bias needs to be borne in mind as we assess the importance of the numerous studies showing that the only important predictors of re-offending are age, sex and the number of previous convictions. Further, it is usually, in this field, impossible to randomise. We are forced to work with clinical samples where different people are already treated differently according to their perceived dangerousness (Buchanan, 1997). Also, no estimate of how often clinicians are right or wrong can properly be made without reference to the time-frame or the rate of occurrence of the behaviour in question.

Within a multidisciplinary approach to discharge there may exist confusion, or perhaps ignorance, of roles and responsibilities. The Audit Commission (1993) recommends that where possible a common patient record, to which all members of the multidisciplinary team have access, should be established. There are problems in proper information sharing (a range of different professionals, forms and files, geographical locations of offices and separate lines of command and a need for urgency when problems do materialise) and failure to share information has often been shown to have led to disastrous results. The Inquiry into the Care of Christopher Clunis (Ritchie, 1994) criticised a number of agencies for failing to pass on information about Mr Clunis' acts of violence. Pursuing and documenting the right process of risk assessment should become everyday practice not only in order to provide adequate clinical care, but also because the civil courts will assume (in relation to negligence litigation) that understanding and pursuing the risk of harm to self *or others* is part of the required standard of ordinary psychiatric clinical practice (Vinestock, 1996). The recommendation (Royal College of Psychiatrists, 1991) that aftercare of 'potentially violent or vulnerable patients' would be facilitated by having 'records stored on computers programmed to bring forward names (for) regular review' is one aspect of the proposals for the introduction of supervision registers (NHS Management Executive, 1994).

Selected findings derived from the review of literature and practice observations indicated the following:

▶ There is confusion over the authority (statutory, professional, hierarchical, personal) of and the individual contributions within the multidisciplinary team.

▶ The number of different records kept for a single patient, together with the diversity of geographical location and electronic and paper formats of records, does not lend itself to the simple and frequent capture of information relevant to the main predictors of risk.

▶ There is general agreement that the predictors used in scales are the right ones, but there is disagreement about the weightings adopted.

▶ The case conference method of the multidisciplinary team does not lend itself to the use of written scales.

▶ Scales may promise much but fail to convince that they can deliver in practice whereas less complex instruments such as checklists may promise less but deliver a practical, widely accepted and cost-efficient aid to risk management.

REFINING THE RESEARCH QUESTIONS

There are a number of issues surrounding the process of refining research questions. For example, although the work for a research degree can be very lengthy and complex it seemed clear that a simple idea had to be at its heart. Putting it another way, if the key issue cannot be summed up in a few sentences, then there is probably a need to focus in even more narrowly on some aspect. Also, any research questions have to be answerable within the constraints of the time and financial resources available. To a great extent it is only possible to get an understanding of good research questions after you make a start on an aspect of the work, a commitment evolves, and research training is undertaken. The processes of reading and of research training quickly make one question the adequacy of early thoughts.

While it is not a difficult matter to find questions such as 'It would be interesting to know if, why, when, or how?' it is not so easy to see how such questions may be answered with any degree of conviction. Also, of necessity many research students will have to work with a very small population of subjects or with small samples of much larger populations. Being able to answer a question about such a small group of subjects may be acceptable but there may be a need or, at the very least, a wish to be able to claim that the findings apply to a much larger group – possibly well beyond the small number taking part in the study. If generalisability is important to them it will be necessary to seek early statistical advice in respect of quantitative data and to read widely about the debate and possible approaches to generalisability of findings from qualitative data (Sapsford and Jupp, 1996; Cramer, 1998; Wright, 1997).

My review of past crisis cases identified many risk factors pertinent to my area of study (Kemshall and Pritchard, 1995 and 1997). For example, statistics have identified that young men are most likely to be perpetrators of violence against another person. Older males are those most at risk of self-harm. Such actuarial factors have been used to develop risk assessment scales for dangerousness (Campbell, 1995) and potential suicide (Bowling, 1991). However, these alone do not guarantee successful prediction of the risk of future harm to others or to self in any *individual* patient. It is widely agreed that assessing the risk of a patient acting in an aggressive or violent way at some time in the future is, at best, an inexact science. The Inquiry into the Case of Kim Kirkham (West Midlands Regional Health Authority, 1991) describes the decision on risk as 'a balanced summary of prediction derived from knowledge of the individual, the present circumstances and what is known of the disorder from which he (or she) is suffering'. Vinestock (1996) emphasises that the information gathering process by the multidisciplinary team is the single most important aspect of the risk assessment. Scott (1977) reminds us that before risk factors are considered they must be gathered and suggests that it is patience, thoroughness and persistence in this process, rather than any diagnostic or interviewing brilliance, that produces results. At the root of this project are questions about how 'risk' information is gathered and translated into 'risk' decisions by multidisciplinary teams operating within limited resources of time, personnel and in-patient beds and against the uncertainties of life in the 'community'. How do professionals go about it? Why do things sometimes go badly wrong? Apart from ever more resources, is there anything which can be done to help the 'risk' decision process get it right more often?

My first idea was to create and test a new risk assessment rating scale. I did not think it would be easy but I did not realise just how difficult such a task would be. My preliminary literature review had informed me about the existence of many different scales in psychiatric practice. The existence of scales specific to risk prediction was, however, unclear. Can scales, measures or other instruments aid this process of gathering and using 'risk' information? In industry, when the results of failure can be catastrophic (both in financial costs and in terms of human lives), we can identify examples of risk assessment at an advanced level. Consider the Dow Fire and Explosion Index (Dickson, 1995), a hazard index which attempts to express the degree of hazard in an objective way by using numbers. When I read in detail about how to devise a rating scale and to test it to prove beyond reasonable doubt that it was measuring what it set out to measure, I quickly had second thoughts about developing one of my own. Testing the validity and reliability of any measuring instrument is a major undertaking but there are, in addition, almost unique methodological problems in testing predictions derived from a mental health scale, particularly in that it is impossible to test on the basis of randomly controlled trials.

At registration for my research it was necessary for me to state clearly the research objectives, albeit that they might have to be revisited and amended as the research progressed. At that stage they were of course only based upon my preliminary search of literature and practice. My original proposal narrowed this to specific objectives: to identify how 'stakeholders' (doctors, nurses, social services, patients, NHS trusts and others) inform the risk assessment process leading to discharge; to discover which standardised risk assessment scales and measures are available; and to carry out analysis and evaluation in order to assess their reliability, extent of use and future potential.

Selecting a supervisor

Having refined my research question to some degree I needed to ensure that I met the criteria of the university in selecting an appropriate supervisor, one that could also support me through relatively uncharted territory in terms of subject, and would ensure support within this strange (to me) culture of the NHS.

One of the biggest problems is that supervisors are in short supply. Firstly, there are university rules regarding the supervision of research degrees. Rules will, for example, specify whether there are to be one or more supervisors and the experience that the supervision 'team' must possess in terms of successfully completed supervisions. The growth in higher education and the emphasis on research output has put pressure on the scarce resource of the experienced supervisor. Most supervisors, if they are good, will have many demands on their time. I was fortunate enough to have as my starting point my then Head of the Department of Risk and Financial Services at Glasgow Caledonian University, Professor John Reid (now semi-retired from the university but still overseeing a number of matters, including my supervision, through to conclusion). Professor Reid's comments on the project are to be found at the end of this chapter. He was able to guide my thinking through many of the theoretical, methodological and practical problems of conducting research. However, it was clear from the early stages that much would be gained by getting additional supervision with experience of health care and the NHS. Professor Jennifer Hunt, Director of the Nursing Research Initiative for Scotland, agreed to become a supervisor and was able to provide me with practical advice on the health service. Professor Hunt's comments are also to be found at the end of this chapter. The appointment of a third supervisor, Professor Catherine Niven of the Department of Nursing and Midwifery at the University of Stirling added a further strength in this area as well as the number of completed PhD supervisions necessary to satisfy the regulations of my university.

Selecting a 'flexible' methodology

I divided the field work into two distinct parts. The first phase was intended to provide, in connection with a substantial literature and practice review, data of sufficient quantity and quality to satisfy the Master of Philosophy phase. More extensive fieldwork yielding richer data is planned for the PhD phase and is described below under 'intended further work'. In broad terms the MPhil phase of fieldwork sought to identify what currently existed in terms of scales, measures and other instruments and to identify the full range of potential contributors to the multidisciplinary team, their frequency of involvement and how their opinions and decisions were recorded. A telephone survey would have been possible other than on the grounds of limited resources. I elected for a postal survey (derived from the literature) of all mental health trusts in the UK and Northern Ireland.

Writers on the subject of research methods stress the need to adopt a professional approach to the conduct of research. Intellectual honesty and integrity lie at the heart of this. This extends to the treatment of subjects even if only with regard to a simple questionnaire. Questions of honest reporting of findings seem to lie mainly with the supervisors, examiners and the researcher, but the impact of research on subjects is governed by a set of rules and an ethics committee – at my university and in most institutions. I was required to explain my plans to gather data by means of a questionnaire. Ethical approval was duly granted and recorded and I will be required to repeat this process to seek approval for the further fieldwork I plan. In addition, it is likely that I will have to submit my plans for individual approval by the ethics committees of those hospitals which I hope will assist me in that further fieldwork. Ethical matters are discussed more fully in Chapter 3.

Conversations with doctors suggested that the medical profession is swamped with questionnaires and that many will simply be put in the dustbin. Turning my attention to ways to maximise the response. I settled on a folded A3 format plus a single page covering letter. In view of the anticipated poor response rate I opted for a census of all relevant NHS trusts rather than merely a sample. There is no standard model of NHS trust and even in 'community and mental health' not all trusts have adult mental health in-patients – the starting point for my research. Careful examination of the Health Service Yearbook identified 185 possibles. I included an opening question designed to allow those trusts without adult in-patients to rule themselves out. The subjects were asked about use of written instruments for risk assessment or management at discharge of adult mental health in-patients in three categories – a hierarchy of increasing complexity: protocol, checklist and rating scale. A specimen of each of these three types (for each, a sheet of pink-coloured A4 paper with text on both sides) was inserted into the questionnaire. Subjects were also asked to identify the categories of personnel contributing information (in person or in writing) at case conferences and to identify the number, location and format of records kept.

My aim was to allow subjects to complete the questionnaire without having to stop and search for figures or for documents. Thus, to obtain some general information on each trust, I wrote to all 185 for a copy of their most recent annual report. From the responses obtained I was able to collect general data such as annual income, patient numbers, range of services and geographical boundaries. The reports varied immensely in quality and content but the sections dealing with mental health services have proved to be a useful additional source of information. Unfortunately, I found that many annual reports did not give me the information I needed, concentrating as they do mainly on the financial report detailing income and expenditure. Rather belatedly, therefore, I turned to the Statistics Divisions of the NHS Executive in Scotland, England, Wales and Northern Ireland in order to build up a profile of each trust which I knew I would need when considering the characteristics of those who responded to my questionnaire and those who did not.

Logically my findings would be most generalisable to the full population of subjects if a large number of the 185 replied; however, I could not automatically assume that those who did not respond were similar to those who did respond. It might be that only those with some specific characteristic were prompted to respond. For example, only those already using risk assessment instruments might have taken the trouble to reply. Those without them may have declined to respond, perhaps because they are unsure what the instruments were all about, or are embarrassed that they cannot report their existence and use. I therefore needed to try to deduce what the non-responders were like. How this is done can become quite complex (Sapsford and Jupp, 1996; Wright, 1997; Cramer, 1998). I chose a range of characteristics to identify in both responders and non-responders to identify if their presence in each group was in similar proportions. The characteristics chosen were annual budget spend on the mental health specialism, the number of in-patient bed days for adult mental health patients (that is excluding geriatric, learning disabilities and child and adolescent categories) and the number of consultant psychiatrists. I am in the process of comparing these characteristics trust by trust for responders and for non-responders. If I find that they follow a broadly similar pattern, it will allow me to claim that conclusions drawn from those who did respond are to a great extent generalisable to the wider population.

THE FINDINGS TO DATE

Fifty-nine subjects (32%) responded to a single mailing. Bear in mind that this is 32% of the population of relevant trusts and not of a sample of some larger population. In other words I have to consider the adequacy of responses to a census rather than to consider the possibility of a sampling error. Although I had hoped for more, I was able to settle for this figure as being sufficient to support findings already largely derived from the literature review and, further, realistically sufficient to permit me to provide evidence of fieldwork for the purpose of writing my application to the university's research degrees committee to seek permission to transfer from MPhil to PhD. A sustained campaign of reminders might have yielded more but would have been time-consuming and may have added only a little to the strength of the findings. Three respondents indicated that their community services did not include adult mental health in-patients; practice varies widely. Most trusts have a discharge protocol or policy and some form of checklist, however, many fewer have a rating scale. Many have instruments in course of development or of piloting. The pattern of attendances at case conferences is similar from trust to trust but the number, location and format of records varies considerably. Patients are sometimes not allowed to be present at case conferences and general practitioners, although invited, hardly ever attend.

The results indicate that the prediction of self-harm or of harm to others is complex and highly inexact. Gut feeling is respected as a complex synthesis of observation and experience but the need for a systematised approach to complement it is recognised. The Care Programme approach and its statutory obligation to record decisions appears to be behind many of the instruments in use. The multidisciplinary team bringing information to the decision-making process is a large shifting number of professionals with different masters, training, professional loyalties and traditions. Psychiatrists remain the key decision-takers though they have had to adapt to working in or with community-based multidisciplinary teams, possibly not led by a psychiatrist. Each patient will generate several different sets of records kept in a variety of formats and locations.

The following points give a flavour of the findings:

▶ 33% were returned by medical directors, 43% by clinical directors, 11% by consultants, with the remainder being delegated to others to return (nurses 5% and managers 2%).

▶ 58% had a protocol, 15% did not and 27% were developing one. 61% had a checklist, 18% did not and 21% were developing one. 36% had a scale, 46% did not and 18% were developing one.

▶ 28 separate categories of people were identified as possible participants at meetings to discuss discharge – from psychiatrists, psychologists and nurses to care home staff, probation officers and police.

▶ 57% of patients were always represented at meetings to discuss discharge, 41% were frequently represented and 2% reported that patients were represented infrequently.

▶ 14% of social workers were always represented at meetings to discuss discharge, 61% were frequently represented, 23% were infrequently represented and 2% were never represented.

▶ 68% of general practitioners were present in person infrequently and 32% were never present at meetings to discuss discharge. 57% of general practitioners were represented in writing infrequently and 47% were never represented in writing.

▶ With regard to the format of psychiatrists' records 23% indicated Separate File Completely, 53% indicated Section in Case File and 6% indicated a combination of Section in Case File and Geographically spread. There were a number of other categories and combinations.

Some respondents used the space for 'Additional comments'. Examples are:

'At Care Programme Approach Reviews (CPA) a scale is used as appropriate rather than routinely.'

'This is simply formalising a process which is part of good clinical practice. It has to be thought about carefully. This will not necessarily be helped by scales or checklists.'

'Our draft Risk Assessment Policy and Guidelines is in final version.'

'We have moved away from using standardised assessment forms and scales for risk. Risk should be assessed at all times and is a continuous process.'

'I know some clinical teams do use protocols, checklists and rating scales. It would be impossible for me to apply these in my own practice – mainly because of the extremely rapid turnover of patients in my acute psychiatric beds.'

'When a high volume of patients is coming and going even five to 10 minutes filling in an extra checklist becomes a great burden on staff.'

'Be careful in your research that you do not answer a very important question in regard to longer-term-stay patients but then apply it to the work of other types of units, for example, the average length of stay in my ward must be about 10 days. Sometimes patients are in and out in 48 hours and follow up is neither possible nor appropriate.'

'We have a questionnaire assessment of risk for all Supervision Register patients and others when necessary.'

TRANSFER FROM MPhil TO PhD

Progression to the PhD phase is by the conduct of empirical research and analysis. It will be qualitative and built around three case studies. At each of three mental health trusts (appropriately selected but essentially dependent upon co-operation) the following methods will be adopted: participant observation of a multidisciplinary team case conference, linked to semi-structured interviews of all members of the multidisciplinary team (whether or not present at conference). I know from my MPhil stage work that it is possible to get access as observer to case conferences and to talk to team members; however, such arrangements will take time and attention to detail in order to set up and will involve ethical approval.

Triangulation will be provided through this use of different methods and different sources and an audit trail will ensure confirmability. Some generalisability of findings may be made if supported by evidence from the three separate case studies together with the additional findings drawn from the MPhil stage survey and the research literature.

Questions to the subjects will probe the practice observed in the MPhil stage work. Instruments actually in use at some hospitals (as identified by the MPhil phase) will be used in the interview method to stimulate discovery of their knowledge and views in order to test the hypotheses. What needs to be demonstrated is some clear contribution to existing knowledge and practice in this field. I cannot prejudge the findings of the next stage of fieldwork, but I anticipate finding evidence to support the following statements:

▶ the value of risk scales in multidisciplinary team-working (for example, removing bias, promotion of logical thought process, ensuring nothing is missed, quick, less training acquired, good defence, information technology compatible);

- the potential disadvantages of scales (for example weightings relevant in one area of UK may be less relevant in others, or they may be used defensively rather than for the benefit of the patient);

- the need for controlled development on a national basis of scales and measures for identification, assessment and control of risk in mental health;

- to point to the changes which must be made to current practice in order to move towards a more systematised and information efficient approach to risk assessment and management.

CHOOSING WHEN TO SAY 'NO'

I believe that research students must be very single-minded in order to be able to devote sufficient time to their research. If my experience is typical, the very fact that I am learning about a specific topic and how to be a researcher means that I have begun to be sought after to join research groups, give presentations, advise students on honours dissertations and the like. I have found that I need to be selective, and only become involved with activities which in some way complement my research and to say 'no' to the others. I have a part-time involvement in a one-year commercially funded piece of research in nursing and risk, including the appointment of a full-time researcher. Also, my contact with Scottish NHS trusts has stimulated the creation of a risk management network for which I act as Chair and Secretary. This is now an established group with the support of most of the Scottish NHS trusts, having to date held six separate seminars throughout Scotland. This has given me access to invaluable contacts within the NHS throughout the UK and in Scotland in particular. However, I have also spent much unproductive time on other matters.

Pursuit of a research degree is a lonely business. With no close team support it would be very easy to get blown off track. A large measure of persistence seems to be required. One consultant psychiatrist responded to my questionnaire by stating that I was poorly informed about current procedures and suggested that I would do well to visit some hospitals and psychiatric units. That came as a bit of a blow as I had in fact already undertaken such visits. However, I decided to write back, politely, thanking him for taking time to respond and ask if I might arrange to visit *his* hospital. A little later his secretary telephoned with some suggested dates – a visit was arranged and it proved to be very worthwhile. Newspaper advertisements for executive appointments often use the expression 'must be a self-starter' meaning, I think, that they must come up with ideas and ways of achieving results rather than simply be excellent about doing the work as instructed by others. Undertaking a research degree certainly requires this quality. I suspect this is true whether the degree is being done on a full- or a part-time basis. Part-time students may have to balance the demands of a 'day job' and family responsibilities but younger full-time research students moving on to a research degree after a good first degree or perhaps a taught masters degree will face the many distractions that go along with that energetic time of life. In future when I see MPhil or PhD after someone's name it will not only tell me that they have studied some subject area in great detail, it will also tell me something about that person's qualities of persistence and self-motivation. I am still enjoying my PhD project and am well motivated to drive it to completion. However, by the time I get near the end I suspect that I will just be glad to see it finished. Not that I plan to give up research – quite the opposite. I already have lots of ideas for further research projects. It will be nice not to have them tied to the process of obtaining a degree.

SUPERVISOR'S COMMENTS
Professor John Reid

My supervisory involvement in Bill Stein's research degree began at the initial stage of formulation of the project. At that time I was the head of the department in which Bill was employed as a lecturer and the prospect of his pursuing a PhD arose out of the regular appraisal discussions – both formal and informal – regarding career and personal development. Bill had been recruited to the department several years earlier after his initial career in insurance, during which he had carried out some part-time teaching for the department. He was keen to enhance his career development prospects and he believed that in his particular circumstances the research degree route was the most appropriate one for him to follow. I concurred and welcomed the prospect of a member of the department achieving the PhD award, as well as the research output (conference papers, publications etc) that could be expected for the Research Assessment Exercise that all universities undergo on a periodic basis.

Whilst the precise regulations and procedures vary from one institution to another, all universities have clearly laid-down guidelines concerning the conduct of higher degrees, including the requirements on supervision. At Glasgow Caledonian University, these guidelines and regulations would appear to be more formal, rigorous and detailed than normal – probably reflecting the need for a 'new' university to be seen to adhere to the highest standards of quality. These regulations require that a suitably experienced and qualified (both in terms of academic subject content and research supervision) team of supervisors be appointed and approved by the university's Research Degrees Committee. One aspect of this is that amongthe supervisory team (usually two, but sometimes three, supervisors) they must have a minimum of two successfully completed PhD supervisions. This can be a significant obstacle in establishing the supervisory team, especially in a discipline that does not have a tradition for study at higher degree level and often requires the appointment of a third supervisor to bring in or top up the necessary number of completions. A further requirement is the appointment of a Director of Studies from among the supervisory team, whose particular function is to 'manage' the project – in terms of ensuring compliance with the regulatory requirements, convening and chairing meetings of supervisors and ensuring that suitable resources (in terms of accommodation, time, computing facilities and required finance) are available for the successful undertaking of the project. Very often, the Director of Studies is the head of the department in which the research degree student is registered.

In Bill's case, at the outset I was a teaching colleague as well as his Head of Department and it was therefore quite easy for us to have frequent, informal discussions about the form his research would take. I had a similar background of experience in insurance and risk management and had a particular research interest in risk management in the public sector. It seemed appropriate, therefore, for me to assume the role of Director of Studies. Being an interdisciplinary project, the supervisory team needed to include at least one supervisor with experience in the field of health and mental illness and from the wide network of contacts in that field that Bill had generated in the process of his initial exploration of the topic area, two were selected who satisfied the scrutiny of the Research Degrees Committee.

My role in Bill's research, as both a supervisor and the Director of Studies, is guiding, directing and motivating his work. Guidance and direction were especially needed in the initial stage of selecting and delineating the project; in other words, ensuring that the expected outcome would be of a status worthy of the award of a PhD, but that the process and methods to be employed would be realistically achievable within the required timescale. The style of supervision (from closely controlled to relatively relaxed) and the need for motivation do of course vary from student to student. In Bill's case, when he embarked upon his research he was already a qualified and experienced professional (in insurance) and as his Head of Department I had evidence of his mature attitude and self-discipline. Accordingly, his supervision has been conducted on a relatively informal basis and the pace of progress has largely been set by himself. What is always important in supervision is that supervisors are regularly provided with the evidence (draft chapters, reports, draft questionnaire and so on) of progress. Bill's professionalism and self-discipline ensured that I have been regularly supplied with the written products of his critical review of the literature and practice, his current thinking and his plans for the next stage of the work.

Whilst the work has progressed smoothly and in a sustained manner, there have been a couple of stages that have called for more intensive interaction between Bill and his supervisors and more direction from them. The first was the submission of his formal application for registration as a MPhil/PhD student, which was achieved at the end of about one year of part-time study. The second was the submission of the application for his registration status to be transferred to PhD. This required a well structured and competently written progress report of about 5,000 words and was completed after a further eighteen months of part-time study. The report contained: a critical analysis of the research literature and professional practice; the specific research questions to be addressed that had been derived from the literature review and the survey of current practice; the methodology to be adopted in addressing the research questions; and the expected outcomes to the research (that is the 'original contribution to knowledge', which is the defining nature of a PhD). The transfer to PhD status was approved, thus giving Bill the 'green light' to progress his research plan with a view to achieving the PhD award within the next two years.

Bill has demonstrated that he has the ability and self-discipline to make satisfactory progress and achieve the targeted milestones *en route* to completion of the work. Regular written reports of work completed will continue to be required by his supervisors and in addition further more intensive periods of interaction will be needed in discussing the results of the fieldwork, the review of the completed written thesis and the preparations for the viva examination.

SUPERVISOR'S COMMENTS
Professor Jennifer Hunt

When I was asked if I would supervise Bill I was happy to do so, both from a personal point of view and also in order to help grow the reputation of the newly established nursing research unit of which I was the Director at the time. I and my senior staff needed to take on supervisory responsibility if we were to be seen as academically credible. Indeed pursuing this was of great importance to my staff since having this on their CVs was crucial to their academic careers.

At Glasgow Caledonian University there are specific regulations regarding the supervision of postgraduate students. Supervisors have to have gained experience working with an experienced supervisor before they are allowed to be the 'senior' supervisor. Rather like nursing, it would also appear that experience gained at one institution is not necessarily transferable to another, which at times can be aggravating. Because I have spent much of my working life within the NHS as a nurse researcher and manager I am, by university standards, an inexperienced supervisor even though my experience of supervising master's and doctoral students stretches over 20 years. I am not therefore Bill's main supervisor but one of a team of three.

I was asked to help supervise Bill because I had a clinical background (nursing) and a knowledge of the care needed by and provided for patients with mental illness. Perhaps of equal value has been my experience in senior management and on national committees dealing with come of the issues which were important to this study and also my range of research experience which enabled me to take a very broad view about approaches, the theoretical background and the methodology.

Bill and I have met, not regularly, but sufficiently often for me to continue to gauge his progress. It is very much up to him to decide when he needs to see me. Working as we do at the same university has made getting together for meetings easier and means that we do meet around the campus from time to time and so, in addition to our formal planned meetings, I can catch up on an informal basis on what is going on and how the work is progressing. Although there are regulations and indeed concepts about supervising, the reality appears to be that the input of the supervisor and the demands made by the student, which may or may not be met, vary enormously. There are no absolute requirements, no prescribed number of meetings as far as I am aware. What actually happens in a supervisory session therefore is very individual depending on the relationship that has developed, on the skills and knowledge of the supervisor and of course their interest in and commitment to providing input to the process.

Bill has been an easy student to supervise. He is very organised, very committed and very persistent. He is willing to listen and take advice but more than able to work independently and get on with the work that needs to be done. To some extent that may be because be is older than many post-graduate students and has learnt to manage his workload and other commitments. He has also been very aware of his lack of knowledge about mental health, psychiatry and the NHS – which is where as a supervisor I have been able to provide needed input. In addition, because his work is on an issue of great topicality and importance to the provision of health care at the present time I have made sure that it has reached those who can make use of it at policy level.

In comparison to some other students I have supervised, he needs less input from me. His problem is that he is at times too meticulous and cautious. This became apparent when he was at the state of needing to get on with his data collection by sending out his questionnaire when he still felt unsure whether it was good enough or should be revised further. A thesis after all is meant to be the work of the student, so advising and supporting are what is required.

It has been interesting to work with someone who comes from a different background and then applies that knowledge to one with which I am so familiar. It has demonstrated once more to me that this kind of cross-pollination can be extremely valuable when it is a genuine drawing together of knowledge and a genuine wish to apply that knowledge objectively.

One aspect of academic supervision that I find somewhat strange is that the different supervisors rarely meet. I met with his main supervisor and Bill himself early on to discuss the whole process but we have never had a meeting of all three supervisors together with or without Bill. I suspect that this is fairly common practice and indeed has been my experience previously.

On the whole the research has gone smoothly. To a large extent this has been due to Bill's ability to manage his work, home and theses commitments. He is also fortunate in that he is less pressured than some doctoral students who are reliant on grants and a more restricted time frame. He has a job, he has support from his departmental head and from his family. But that should not detract from his achievement in getting such a well-designed study under way and being willing to take a risk of studying an environment with which he was unfamiliar – and by taking that risk, adding real value to both disciplines.

REFERENCES

Audit Commission (1993) *What Seems to Be the Matter: Communication between Hospitals and Patients.* London: HMSO.

Bell, J. (1993) *Doing Your Research Project.* Buckingham: Open University Press.

Blaxter, L., Hughes, C., Tight, M. (1996) *How to Research.* Buckingham: Open University Press.

Bowling, A. (1991) *Measuring Health: a Review of Quality of Life Measurement Scales.* Milton Keynes: Open University Press.

Buchanan, A. (1997) The investigation of acting on delusions as a tool for risk assessment in the mentally disordered. *British Journal of Psychiatry;* 170 (suppl. 32): 12–16.

Campbell, J.C. (ed.) (1995) *Assessing Dangerousness: Violence by Sexual Offenders, Batterers and Child abusers.* London: Sage Publications.

Carson, D. (1991) Risk-taking in mental disorder. In: Carson, D. (ed.) *Risk-taking in Mental Disorder; Analyses, Policies and Practical Strategies.* Chichester: SLE Publications.

Carson, D. (1994) Dangerous people; through a broader conception of 'risk' and 'danger' to better decisions. *Expert Evidence;* 3: 51–69.

Cormack, D.F.S. (ed.) (1996) *The Research Process in Nursing.* Oxford: Blackwell Science.

Cramer, D. (1998) *Fundamental Statistics for Social Research.* London: Routledge.

Denscombe, M. (1998) *The Good Research Guide.* Buckingham: Open University Press.

Dickson, G.C.A., Gassidy, D., Gordon, A.W., et al (1995) *Risk Management.* London: Chartered Insurance Institute.

Grounds, A. (1995) Risk assessment and management in clinical context. In: Chrichton, J. (ed) *Psychiatric Patient Violence: Risk and Response.* London: Duckworth.

Holloway, I., Wheeler, S. (1996) *Qualitative Research for Nurses.* Oxford: Blackwell Science.

Holloway, I. (1997) *Basic Concepts for Qualitative Research.* Oxford: Blackwell Science.

Hughes, J. (1990) *The Philosophy of Social Research.* London: Longman.

Hussey, J., Hussey, R. (1997) *Business Research.* London: Macmillan Press.

Kemshall, H., Pritchard, J. (eds.) (1995) *Good Practice in Risk Assessment and Risk Management*. London: Jessica Kingsley Publishers.

Kemshall, H., Pritchard, J. (eds.) (1997) *Good Practice in Risk Assessment and Risk Management 2. Protection, Rights and Responsibilities*. London: Jessica Kingsley Publishers.

Lipsedge, M. (1995) Psychiatry: reducing risk in clinical practice. In: Vincent, C. (ed.) *Clinical Risk Management*. London: British Medical Journal Publishing Group.

Monaghan, J. (1993) Mental disorder and violence: another look. In: Hodgins, S. (ed.) *Mental Disorder and Crime*. London: Sage Publications.

Moore, B. (1995) *Risk Assessment: A Practitioner's Guide to Predicting Harmful Behaviour*. London: Whiting and Birch.

National Audit Office (1996) *Health and Safety in NHS Acute Hospital Trusts in England*. London: The National Audit Office.

NHS Management Executive (1994) *Introduction of Supervision Registers for Mentally Ill People*. Heywood: DoH.

North West London Mental Health NHS Trust (1994) *Report of the Independent Panel of Inquiry Examining the Case of Michael Buchanan*. London: NW London Mental Health NHS Trust.

Phillips, E.M., Pugh, D.S. (1987) *How to Get a PhD*. Buckingham: Open University Press.

Potts, J. (1995) Risk assessment and management; a home office perspective. In: Chrichton, J. (ed.) *Psychiatric Patient Violence: Risk and Response*. London: Duckworth.

Reed, J. (1997) Risk assessment and clinical risk management: the lessons from recent enquiries. *British Journal of Psychiatry;* 170 (suppl. 32): 4–7.

Ritchie, J.H. (Chairman) (1994) *Report of the Inquiry into the Care and Treatment of Christopher Clunis*. London: HMSO.

Roberts, G., Holly, J. (1996) *Risk Management in Healthcare*. London: Institute of Risk Management.

Royal College of Psychiatrists (1991) *Good Medical Practice in the Aftercare of Potentially Violent or Vulnerable Patients Discharged from In-patient Psychiatric Treatment*. Council Report CR12. London: Royal College of Psychiatrists.

Sapsford, R., Jupp, V. (eds.) (1996) *Data Collection and Analysis*. London: Sage Publications.

Scott, P.D. (1977) Assessing dangerousness in criminals. *British Journal of Psychiatry*; 131: 12–142.

Vinestock, M. (1996) Risk assessment. 'A word to the wise'? *Advances in Psychiatric Treatment;* 2: 3–10.

Walshe, K., Dineen, M. (1998) *Clinical Risk Management: Making a Difference?* London: NHS Confederation.

Dick, D., Shuttleworth, B., Charlton, J. (1991) *Report of the Panel of Inquiry Appointed to Investigate the Case of Kim Kirkman.* Birmingham: West Midlands Health Authority.

Wright, D.B. (1997) *Understanding Statistics. An Introduction for the Social Sciences.* London: Sage Publications.

7. Building bridges between nursing research and practice

Author
Maureen Coombs

Commentary
Helen Bartlett

INTRODUCTION

'A little knowledge that acts is worth infinitely
more than much knowledge that is idle.'

Khalil Gibran

The importance of inquiry within nursing was first recognised by Florence
Nightingale in the 1860s (Nightingale, 1980). Since that time, the nursing role, the
context of nursing and the society within which nurses practise have continued
to develop. Although contemporary nursing has evolved from Nightingale's vision,
what has become of the legacy regarding the significance of inquiry?

In 1996 the Foundation of Nursing Studies (FoNS, 1996a) published details of a
qualitative, evaluative study resulting from workshops held to explore and
implement research within the delegates' own practice base. Comments made by
delegates regarding their perceptions on research included 'done by them and not
us', 'lack of understanding', 'not relevant', 'trendy' and 'extra effort'. These were
contrasted with views including 'groundbreaking', 'innovative' and 'desire to be
involved'. I think we have to question why this paradox continues to exist and
what has become of nursing's research legacy.

The aim of this chapter is to explore the issues central to the dissemination and
uptake of research in practice. The literature will initially be examined to explore
the arguments for why nursing should be research-based. Barriers to research
implementation will be examined and innovative strategies to promote research
utilisation will then be discussed. There already exists substantive literature in all
these areas. Whilst drawing on this, personal experience as a practising clinical
nurse currently undertaking doctoral studies will be used to provide a personal
perspective. This chapter will conclude with suggested priorities for the future in
order to build bridges between research and practice.

NURSING: WHY A RESEARCH-BASED PROFESSION?

In exploring why nursing should be researched-based, the main arguments appear to be related to the nature of nursing knowledge and its ability to underpin practice. Within this, research is seen as a planned, systematic search for information, with the purpose of increasing the body of nursing knowledge (Goode et al, 1987). Chater (1975) asserts that nursing should be based on scientific principles and patient care should be based on defensible research-based findings (Bergman, 1990). Indeed, it has been suggested that not to base nursing practice on research is unethical (Styles, 1982). With such a challenge placed at the door of practitioners, it is unsurprising that Sheehan (1986) sees the application of research findings as being a major challenge to the development of nursing. In trusts and clinical units we have witnessed a growing demand to develop a research culture in order to improve patient care and service delivery. This has been reinforced by recent NHS research and development strategies (DoH, 1993; DoH, 1995), culminating in the new appointment of a part-time professor of nursing research at the Department of Health in 1998 (Garbett, 1998).

A further argument put forward in the nursing literature describes a strong research base existing alongside professional autonomy and professional recognition. Research has been seen to be an important aspect in the advancement of the nursing profession (Thomas, 1985), in the empowerment of nurses (Titchen et al, 1993) and in strengthening the professional base of nursing (Hopps, 1994). This has involved discussions regarding the use of unique or eclectic knowledge in developing a nursing knowledge base and its importance in demonstrating value to health care colleagues (Akinsanya, 1994). These debates have subsequently been mirrored in the content of professional codes of conduct (UKCC, 1992) and in professional education (ENB, 1989).

The development of a research culture in nursing has only gained momentum in recent times. Nurses were probably the last professional group to demonstrate an active interest in researching nursing! After initial study by sociologists in the 1950s, the government undertook work on the deployment of nursing staff in acute hospitals between 1963 and 1965. The results demonstrated wide variations in staff levels and absence of quality of care measures. From this, a nursing officer post with special responsibility for developing research was subsequently created. The first attempt by nurses to examine nursing problems arose from the 1966 Royal College of Nursing study to develop measures for quality of nursing care (Inman, 1975). This was soon followed by the Briggs Committee report (DHSS, 1972) which further reinforced the need for research-based practice and provided the 'mantra, carrot and stick' for nursing to become a research-based profession (Salvage, 1998).

Since that time there have been many developments and opportunities for increasing nursing research. For example, the establishment of the Steinberg Collection at the Royal College of Nursing, the National Health Service (NHS) Centre for Reviews and Dissemination, the Cochrane Centre and the Centre for Evidence-Based Nursing at York, all provide important sources of reference for research and systematic reviews. Provision of resources to implement nursing research varies, although the Foundation of Nursing Studies plays a significant role here.

Despite the intense focus on nursing research, there has been little evaluation of the usefulness and relevance of completed research (Bircumshaw, 1990). Studies have revealed that the peak of research activity occurs approximately 20 years before its impact on the workplace (Morgan, 1985) and this poor uptake by clinical nurses in the UK has been widely documented in the literature. Veeramah's (1995) exploratory study assessed mental health nurses' attitudes and needs in relation to the use of research findings. The study revealed that the majority of nurses had a positive attitude to research, but very few actually used research findings. These findings are reiterated in Camiah's case study with pre- and post-registration students (1997), and Meah and colleagues' qualitative research with midwives (1996).

Reviewing the literature, it becomes apparent that this is not just an issue encountered by the UK. Wright (1996) sampled 40 medical-surgical and psychiatric nurses in acute and primary care in Sydney, Australia with a non-randomised questionnaire. Some interesting disparities were revealed in the results. Although 91% of the sample thought that research was necessary for practice, only 73% saw the need for research in their area. Twenty per cent did not want further research information. The poor uptake of nursing research and a lack of knowledge were similarly revealed in Sweden (Kajermo et al, 1998). Interestingly, this work also highlighted a problem with translation and comprehension of the predominant language used in publishing research – English.

It is frequently argued that research findings cannot be directly imported from other cultures. The UK study by Dunn et al (1998) illustrates this through the use of the BARRIERS scale, an instrument developed in the USA. This scale focuses on key factors influencing research utilisation (nurses, setting, research qualities and presentation). Using a convenience sample of 316 nurses, the items on the scale were consistently perceived as strong or negligible across the two countries. The main cross-cultural differences were related to the nurses' confidence in evaluating research and their perceptions of their authority to change practice.

This problem of care and treatment remaining largely unaffected by research (Walshe et al, 1995) is not, however, unique to nursing. In medicine, only one in five interventions have been shown to be based on rigorous evidence (Smith, 1991), with clinical decisions continuing to be based on distant primary training or personal interpretations (Smith, 1993). Similar problems have also have been reported in physiotherapy (Newham, 1997) and occupational therapy (Short-DeGraff, 1997).

BARRIERS TO RESEARCH IN PRACTICE

So what prevents the dissemination and uptake of research? Many approaches have been taken to explore this issue ranging from rhetoric and debate, to theoretical and philosophical. Brown (1995) for example, uses a communication model to illustrate why expressed beliefs and actual behaviour in research and practice are so discongruent. Crane (1985) uses diffusion models to explore research dissemination and utilisation. In her very pragmatic and forward thinking paper, Davis (1981) details her experiences as Associate Chief, Nursing Service for Research in the University of California. In this she states that the key issues affecting the introduction of research to be as much organisational and cultural as they are methodological and technical. Whilst she does not define the term 'technical', I think that the remaining three domains provide a valuable framework with which to explore the literature.

Organisational barriers

The organisational barriers to research utilisation discussed here are mainly concerned with the service organisation. Some educational and policy organisational factors do exist but are considered later as they arise more within the cultural and methodological context. Organisational obstacles to utilising research include heavy workloads and lack of time (Hanson, 1994), lack of funds and reward, lack of peer, administrative and physician support (Bowie, 1981) and lack of autonomy (Lacey, 1994). This has resulted in negative attitudes from practising nurses to research. The support from managers with authority to provide the resources (time, funding and personnel) necessary for research and its uptake are also seen as important organisational issues (Lo-Biondo-Woods and Haber, 1994).

Utilising research findings is a highly complex task requiring a positive attitude and an ongoing interest to establish a research culture (Closs and Cheater, 1994). Research awareness does not implicitly mean research mindedness but continuing education can encourage the uptake of research in practice (Dickson, 1996). The philosophy of the ward (Parahoo, 1988) and the experience and motivation of staff (Mulhall, 1995) can all affect research implementation.

A contemporary view of perceptions to research can be found in a study undertaken by Bartlett et al (1997) which retrospectively identified the nursing research activity within an NHS trust over a six-year period. In the study, the difficulty of gaining comprehensive information was highlighted. The main reasons for this were related to practitioner uncertainty regarding the use of the terms audit, research or practice development. In addition, no infrastructure existed within the trust to disseminate research findings and assistance with the development of a database was not given priority; these factors worked to hinder access to the information.

For me, this study highlights some of the key issues to be addressed in order for service and clinical staff to support research activities and invest in a research culture. My own clinical experiences in intensive care reveal that, no matter how great the aspirations to ensure that practice is research-based, in reality the clinical pace and therefore workload demands on practitioners remain. Even working in a supportive unit, the harsh reality is that after several cost-saving exercises, eventually and regrettably, the only 'fat' to be trimmed is that which was originally intended to support practice development, the prime objective of service understandably being to provide patient care. It appears that the current, much publicised national nursing shortage only serves to place greater demand on clinical nurses and reduces the time, energy and enthusiasm available to develop research-based practice.

Most of the solutions to research in practice focus on the shortcomings of individual nurses (Tornquist, 1995) but I would agree with Funk et al (1991) who comment that perceived organisational powerlessness is an important factor in preventing research utilisation. There needs to be debate at all levels regarding the contribution that research can make to health care and the resources that are needed for this. Even with creative and resourceful senior nursing staff, unless the creation and maintenance of a research culture are supported and invested in by general management and the trust structure, the situation will not change. Nursing would do well to look outside its own profession to see what lessons could be learnt from medical colleagues who would appear to have resources and recognition for research built in to their career structures and, for some, into their working day.

There are a few basic strategies which have been successfully used to address some of these organisational restrictions including the use of journal clubs (Tibbles et al, 1994); research focus groups (Davis, 1981); research newsletters (Pettengill et al, 1994); greater access to library facilities and information technology sources (Bostrum and Wise, 1994); and support from experienced research nurses (Dufault et al, 1995). A more formalised reward and financial system, even through the granting of research release time or paid leave, would support greater research activity. This could be built into individual performance review and related to professional role responsibilities (Davis, 1981). A more robust infrastructure at trust level is needed to achieve greater co-ordination and dissemination of research projects through the directorates and more thorough monitoring of the nursing contribution to trusts' research and development activities (Bartlett et al, 1997). Through such strategies research will increasingly be perceived by all as a legitimate activity.

Cultural barriers

The organisational issues, however, may not be fully resolved until the cultural issues are addressed. Hicks and Hennessy (1995) suggests that there has been an absence of academic discipline within nursing and therefore a lack of research tradition. This has led to a disinclination towards any role responsibility not firmly rooted in direct caring activities. The current attitude towards research is therefore the legacy of a vocational and not an academic culture in nursing.

The absence of an established academic tradition manifests itself in many ways. Bassett (1992) identifies a lack of educational background and preparation in clinical practice. This deficiency leads to a dearth of research knowledge (Goode et al, 1987) and therefore an ignorance of research terminology (Hunt, 1987) by clinical nurses. In addition, it has been suggested that researchers have investigated topics of personal interest and not those necessarily perceived as a priority by the profession (Dracup and Weinberg, 1983). Quite simply, a strong relationship has never been established between the producers of research and potential users (Watt, 1993); nurses perceive research as being detached from the real world (Wright et al, 1996) and therefore question its relevance to practice (Akinsanya, 1994).

For many, access to research is through the nursing journals. There has been a dramatic increase in nursing journals and studies over the past twenty years. Four hundred and thirty journals concerned with nursing and nurses were listed in a 1993–1994 periodical (Cullum and Sheldon, 1995). Nursing journals are considered to have contributed to professional nursing and to documenting the body of nursing knowledge (Smith, 1996). However, in the study by Stephens et al (1992) about library skills in nurses, 50% of 77 nurse participants had not visited a library in the previous six months. A further issue is that researchers and educators are encouraged to publish their research findings in peer-reviewed journals to enhance their department's rating in the Higher Education Funding Council's research assessment exercise and yet these journals are not read on a regular basis by the majority of nurses (Webb, 1990). For research to be used in practice by practitioners, it needs to be published in a comprehensible language for the target audience. Perhaps the key question to ask is who is the intended target audience, as some feel that nurse researchers fail to ask the questions that practitioners need to have answered (Mulhall, 1995).

In a report by Yorkshire Health Authority (1991), it is argued that much research is undertaken primarily for academic courses and not in order to influence practice. The language used may therefore be inappropriate for the target audience. In addition, only one in 16 nurses submit papers after their courses for publication (Hicks, 1995). The reasons given for this include lack of time to publish and lack of confidence in the instrument used in the work. Despite concerns regarding sample size and the representativeness of Hick's sample group, these results still raise questions regarding the validity of such nursing courses and the rigour of the course research undertaken.

It would appear to me, standing with 'a foot in both camps', that there are almost two different worlds (Haines and Jones, 1994), that are governed by different rules and language. In order to bring these two worlds of practice and academia together, there needs to be an appreciation of each other's worlds, clarification of what can and cannot be achieved and a sharing of responsibilities to fulfil this. For example, if we agree that individual practitioners have a responsibility to demonstrate research-based practice, then educators also have a responsibility to integrate research into their teaching and to develop critical appraisal skills in their students (Smith, 1993). Perhaps as more nurses are exposed to higher education, sensitivity to research issues may increase (Hopps, 1994).

One point worth exploring here concerns the nature of research dissemination and utilisation. Dissemination of research is part of the process that leads to research utilisation. However, it has been argued that to date diffusion has been used to process research information, diffusion being a haphazard and random process (Dickson, 1996). What is needed is a move towards dissemination using a planned and targeted approach (Lomas, 1994). The emphasis on undertaking research has often been placed on the research process and not on the dissemination of the results. Researchers continue to fail to market and disseminate research findings in an understandable way (Cullum and Sheldon, 1996) and there continues to be no formal research implementation strategy with little formal infrastructure at any level (FoNS, 1996b).

If policy-makers are seriously concerned with health care being research-based, then research dissemination should be required as an indicator of performance. Researchers would then have a responsibility to produce defensible findings, emphasising implications for practice and disseminate their research findings to ensure that the research is accessible to practice (McIntosh, 1995).

Perhaps the final point to raise here concerns fostering, as Davis (1981) puts it, 'a research posture'. This entails a review of nurses' role in research and how nurses undertake research. The nursing role in health care research can be diverse: from undertaking a study at master's and doctoral level or supporting colleagues' research studies, to collecting samples and data for studies at unit level. Having gained personal experience in all these areas, one issue becomes clear: research studies involving the patient lie within the domain of the medical establishment. The procedures for access to patients are via the medical organisation and Research Ethics Committee. Anecdotal evidence suggests that such committees have a tendency to be dominated by a large percentage of medical personnel and often have only one nurse representative. The response by the medical establishment to nursing research has been reported to lie on a continuum from indifference to hostility (Lacey, 1994). The predominant research paradigm of positivism continues and is reflected by the high profile of randomised controlled trials in local and national research databases. This has consequently led to a lack of consensus over the definition and design of research within non-medical groups (Hicks, 1997).

Methodological barriers

Historically, the dominant model of research is the biomedical model (Davis, 1981). Nursing and other health care professions have therefore had to compete with the dominant clinical-service orientation and values of medicine. Constraints on resources at all levels in the research utilisation process are apparent, with inter-professional problems and uni-professional domination (FoNS, 1996b). This has had an impact on research methods and funding, with consequences for the quality and quantity of nursing research available.

Drawing on my own experience undertaking clinical ethnography, the sample of medical staff interviewed, whilst being extremely co-operative and generous with their time, have demonstrated a range of reactions to the research approach used. Some have been bemused, some entered into academic debate, while some were sceptical that the study could be a rigorous, scientific process. Nurses, like physiotherapists, are eclectic in the research methods used (Ekdahl et al, 1998) and an insight into their respective cultures is required to understand this (O'Connor, 1995). It is hoped that the continuing growth of multidisciplinary studies will ensure that all forms of inquiry are critically evaluated (Short-De Graff, 1994). It will be interesting to see if the adoption of evidence-based health care and clinical governance will acknowledge the complementary nature of all forms of inquiry.

The majority of nursing research continues to be undertaken by individuals, is small scale, not related to any global research strategy and poorly funded (Hicks, 1995). Historically, research funding has been allocated to medically driven quantitative research projects (Parahoo, 1988). This has meant that nurses, without a track record of success, are faced with a highly competitive field (Hancock, 1993). The situation is gradually changing with specific awards being ring-fenced by the Medical Research Council (Newham, 1997) and health services research funding being allocated to studies of direct relevance to patient care (Mead, 1996). It is therefore important that nursing maintains its profile in, its contribution to and political awareness of the NHS research and development agenda (Tierney, 1998).

ON BUILDING BRIDGES

So how can research dissemination and utilisation be optimised within the nursing profession? How can the bridges between research and practice be built? What key principles should be considered? Innovative roles (Bond, 1996); innovative nursing units (Vaughan and Edwards, 1995); and innovative research strategies, including the use of action research (Titchen and Binnie, 1993), have all been used in an attempt to bring practice and research closer together. However, few of these have ever been comprehensively evaluated (Kitson et al, 1996).

Kitson et al. (1996) describe a framework which for me addresses the key barriers raised in the literature and attempts to integrate research and development with practice. It is argued by Kitson that traditionally, deductively tested knowledge has been given to practitioners to use, ignoring the inductive elements of context, experience and interpretation. Acknowledging these weaknesses, the framework develops an integrated practice development model. Knowledge is generated by inductive description and deductive hypothesis testing. The resultant theory is then tested through research activity and systematic reviews and is then formally evaluated after its implementation. The strength of this model is the equal significance placed on the inductive approach and the importance placed on interpersonal and facilitation skills. Researchers work democratically and collaboratively with staff on changing practice, thereby ensuring that the practitioner is an integral part of the rigorous describing, analysing and action research cycle. Surely this is important if research and practice are to be integrated?

This model, although not formally evaluated to date, appears to offer a shared, collaborative approach to research and practice development. In addition, the model's principles could be applied to any level of research development from national policy to clinical unit level and incorporate any research paradigm, organisational role or disciplinary orientation. Stocking (1992) asserts that research utilisation is an organisational *not* an individual responsibility. I would suggest that research utilisation is an organisational *and* individual responsibility; this is what I perceive Kitson's model to address. Through its implementation, nursing could move beyond the current culture of analysis and blame (Tornquist, 1995) to address and reinforce some of the organisational, cultural and methodological opportunities highlighted in this chapter with the goal of increasing research utilisation and strengthening the research commitment.

The conclusion then, on assimilating this substantial body of literature is that the development of a research culture is multi-factorial (Rodgers, 1994) and contextually dependent (Closs and Cheater, 1994). If we are ever to maximise the potential of research in practice we must move beyond the difference individuals can make (MacGuire, 1990). Conflicts and contradictions must be reduced and commitment must be fostered at all levels. The lack of planning and cohesion that has dominated the research arena is possibly responsible for the current situation in which research is driven by economic, in addition to social and professional concerns. This has consequences for how research findings are translated into action and the agenda for change that directs practitioners, educationists, managers and policy-makers. It may be against this backdrop that the strongest impetus for change will occur and consumers of the service may become the lever for change. Traditionally, established academic groups have set the research agenda. In the future, policy instruments and financial levers may be used to increase the uptake of research (DoH, 1995).

There needs to be a higher professional commitment to research by practitioners; increased facilitation of research and its application by educationists; specific dissemination strategies clearly articulated by researchers; increased resourcing in its broadest sense by managers; and improved collaboration between different policy-making arenas. The research paradigm needs to be expanded to incorporate and appreciate multi-method and multi-professional research. This must occur in conjunction with discussion about the nature and purpose of research which, in this current market-driven health care system, should be to improve the effectiveness and quality of the service provided.

Health care professions do not share the same starting point for their research base. Medical research spans over four hundred years, since the publication of Versalius' anatomy book in 1543 (Sheehan, 1986). In her 1987 paper on nursing research, Hunt believed nursing research to be 15 years old at that time. Nursing has made comparatively good progress – but much is yet to be achieved. In building bridges, there needs to be a shared vision, a shared language, shared tools and responsibilities agreed by all to ensure that strong and lasting bridges are built.

SUPERVISOR'S COMMENTS
Helen Bartlett

Much has been written about the dissemination and utilisation of nursing research in practice and in this chapter we are provided with a comprehensive summary of the issues and debates by a doctoral student with a 'foot in both camps'. As a senior nurse seconded full-time to undertake her doctorate, Maureen Coombs argues that the responsibility for research dissemination and utilisation is both an organisational and an individual one. While Maureen's experiences reveal some frustrations, her analysis of the situation reflects the growing maturity and empowerment of the profession, leaving behind the debates that have only served to highlight the dependency culture and self-destructive tendencies of nursing. Maureen suggests that educationists, researchers, managers, practitioners and policy makers all have a role to play and that users will increasingly act as levers for change. As an ethnographer studying policy-making in intensive care, Maureen is well placed to comment on the strengths and weaknesses of the nurse's contribution and identify areas for development. While some of the perspectives in this chapter are not new, a wide range of issues on the dissemination and use of research in practice are highlighted. This commentary focuses on some key aspects of Maureen's analysis from a supervisor's perspective.

First, Maureen stresses the need for researchers to articulate plans for dissemination. This is an important message for researchers at any level. So many dissertations and theses are left unpublished and supervisors could do more to help students plan to disseminate their work. During her time as a research student, Maureen has broadened her dissemination horizons considerably and has not only presented papers locally within her speciality, but also at the RCN Research Society Annual Conference and an international conference in Australia. Opportunities to present seminars within the school and a paper at the school's research conference, have provided a safe and constructive environment for gaining experience. Like many other research students, Maureen initially worried whether her work was of sufficient standing for the wider conference arena, but her confidence has steadily grown as her studies have progressed. She also highlights the need to disseminate research findings at an organisational level and should be in a good position to help create appropriate forums to facilitate this when she returns to her employing trust.

Second, the need for academics to make their research more accessible is raised. In the preparation of this chapter, we discussed the problems faced by research students in achieving this. Doctoral training focuses on the development of scholarly writing, often to the detriment of a more accessible style. In her role as student representative on the School Research Committee, Maureen has made me more aware of the issue of language generally by commenting that she found the jargon and content of meetings to be quite impenetrable. It is important to be reminded that a research culture can become too exclusive and that we must constantly seek ways of keeping it accessible to both clinicians and students. Supervisors also need to recognise that it is important for research students to develop a repertoire of writing styles that can be geared appropriately to different audiences. Maureen acknowledged that she found it quite difficult to approach this chapter in a more personal style and this probably reflects the constraints imposed on research students by the development of scholarly writing.

Third, Maureen argues for increased resources at the organisational level to support research and its dissemination. Many areas are mentioned, but 'support from experienced researchers' is worthy of further examination. Research leadership has to be the key to developing a research culture. There are many advantages to be observed from Maureen's location in the School's Research Centre during her studies. She has perhaps not experienced the isolation of which many research students complain. Her supervisors, fellow research students and the centre's research staff have a common agenda and the exchange of ideas and mutual support flows from this research culture. Importantly, Maureen and other research students have become a resource to some of the teaching staff who are less research active. Achieving this in the trust environment is a bigger challenge as research centres or career pathways are uncommon. If research activity is to be promoted and sustained, a research leadership role will need to be more clearly defined in the remit of senior practitioners and responsibility for managing research will need to be taken by the nursing directorates. Partnerships with local universities can be a very fruitful way of supporting this development. Senior clinicians with research training such as Maureen will be well equipped as role models and leaders within trusts. Her full-time secondment is an example of what can be achieved and is a demonstration of real organisational commitment. We should not forget, however, that strong personal motivation is an essential requirement of any research activity and, in the case of full-time research students, some sacrifices on the financial and social fronts are inevitable.

Fourth, Maureen's experiences reveal that qualitative methods continue to be questioned as a valid method. She describes the suspicion that her ethnographic methods aroused in the medical profession during her fieldwork, particularly in relation to scientific rigour. The early stages of Maureen's supervision were designed to prepare her to deal with such scepticism as she was vigorously challenged to defend the use of an ethnographic approach. Although she does not suggest in this chapter how her own research might influence practice, Maureen recommends the use of a model that integrates research and practice. It is perhaps difficult for research students at the writing-up stage to take themselves beyond the intrinsic fascination of their data and consider how their findings might be utilised in practice. The debate around different research paradigms will no doubt continue in the health care arena and meanwhile research students have to become proficient in their methodology, demonstrating a systematic and sound approach.

Finally, it is gratifying to see that underpinning Maureen's analysis is an appreciation of the need to locate any discussion about research utilisation and dissemination in a wider policy context. Informed by the emerging findings from her study, she calls for improvements in the collaboration between policy-making agencies. It can be extremely difficult for doctoral students engaged in a narrow field of study to keep abreast of the wider political and policy issues in their discipline. However, the politics of research are hard to ignore in a school that is focused on improving its research rating in the next Higher Education Funding Council research assessment exercise! Full-time students perhaps pick up these issues more quickly than those undertaking studies in a part-time capacity. A doctoral training should help prepare nurses to engage themselves in the wider NHS research and development agenda.

Writing this chapter has been a timely experience for both student and supervisor. We had several discussions about the need for Maureen's writing to be bolder and to draw more on personal experience. This highlights for me a gap in the preparation of our research students and has focused attention on a number of important areas to be considered in the writing-up phase.

REFERENCES

Akinsanya, J.A. (1994) Making research useful to the practising nurse. *Journal of Advanced Nursing*; 19: 174–179.

Bartlett, H., Ersser, S., Davies, C. et al (1997) Characteristics and dissemination of nursing research in an acute healthcare trust. *Nursing Times Research*; 2: 6, 414–422.

Bassett, C. (1992) The integration of research in the clinical setting: obstacles and solutions. A review of the literature. *Nursing Practice*; 6: 1, 4–8.

Bergman, R. (1990) Priorities in nursing research change and continuity. In: Bergman, R. (ed.) *Nursing Research for Nursing Practice*. London: Chapman and Hall.

Bircumshaw, D. (1990) The utilisation of research findings in clinical nursing practice. *Journal of Advanced Nursing*; 15: 1272–1280.

Bond, S. (1996) Forging links between academia and practice through research. *Nursing Standard*; 10: 27, 43–45.

Bostrom, J., Wise, L. (1994) Closing the gap between research and practice. *Journal of Nursing Administration*; 24: 5, 22–27.

Bowie, K. (1981) Implementing research in clinical settings. *Association of Operating Room Nurses*; 33: 1075–1077.

Brown, G.D. (1995) Understanding barriers to basing nursing practice upon research: a communication model approach. *Journal of Advanced Nursing*; 21: 154–157.

Camiah, S. (1997) Utilisation of nursing research in practice and application strategies to raise research awareness amongst nurse practitioners: a model for success. *Journal of Advanced Nursing*; 26: 1193–1202.

Chater, S. (1975) *Understanding Research in Nursing*. Geneva: World Health Organization (WHO).

Closs, S.J., Cheater, F.M. (1994) Utilisation of nursing research: culture, interest and support. *Journal of Advanced Nursing*; 19: 762–773.

Crane, J. (1985) Using research in practice. Research utilisation: theoretical perspectives. *Western Journal of Nursing Research*; 7: 2, 261–268.

Cullum, N., Sheldon, T. (1996) Clinically challenged. *Nursing Management*; 3: 4, 14–16.

Davis, M.Z. (1981) Promoting nursing research in the clinical setting. *Journal of Nursing Administration*; 11: 3, 22–27.

Department of Health and Social Security (1972) *Report of the Committee on Nursing* (Briggs report). London: HMSO.

Department of Health (1993) *Report of the Taskforce on the Strategy for Research in Nursing, Midwifery and Health Visiting.* London: HMSO.

Department of Health (1995) *Methods to Promote the Implementation of Research Findings in the NHS: Priorities for Evaluation. Report to the NHS Central Research and Development Committee, October 1995.* Leeds: DoH.

Dickson, R. (1996) Dissemination and implementation: the wider picture. *Nurse Researcher*; 4: 1, 5–13.

Dracup, K., Weinberg, S.L. (1983) Another case for nursing research. *Heart and Lung*; 12: 3.

Dufault, M.A., Bielecki, C., Collins, E. et al (1995) Changing nurses' pain assessment practice: a collaborative research utilisation approach. *Journal of Advanced Nursing*; 21: 634–645.

Dunn, V., Crichton, N., Roe, B. et al (1998) Using research for practice: a UK perspective of the BARRIERS Scale. *Journal of Advanced Nursing*; 26: 1203–1210.

Ekdahl, C., Nilstun, T. (1998) Paradigms in physiotherapy research: an analysis of 68 Swedish doctoral dissertations. *Physiotherapy Theory and Practice;* 14: 159–169.

English National Board (1989) *Management of Change in Education.* London: ENB.

Foundation of Nursing Studies (1996a) *Breaking Down Barriers: Effective Implementation of Research. A Report of an Evaluation of a Series of Workshops.* London: FoNS.

Foundation of Nursing Studies (1996b) *The Utilisation of Research in Nursing: A Report of a Phenomenological Atudy Involving Nurses and Managers.* London: FoNS.

Funk, S.G., Champagne, M.T., Wiese, R.A. et al, (1991) Barriers to using research findings in practice: the clinician's perspective. *Applied Nursing Research*; 4: 2, 90–95.

Garbett, R. (1998) The chance to fight nursing's corner at the department. *Nursing Times Research*; 3: 1, 71.

Gibran, K. (1965) *A Third Treasury of Khalil Gibran.* New Jersey: Citadel.

Goode, C.J., Lovett, M.K., Hayes, J.E. et al (1987) Use of research based knowledge in clinical practice. *Journal of Nursing Administration;* 17: 12, 11–18.

Haines, A., Jones, R. (1994) Implementing findings of research. *British Medical Journal*; 308: 1488–1492.

Hancock, C. (1993) Promoting research: the RCN's role. *Nurse Researcher*; 1: 2, 72–80.

Hanson, J.L. (1994) Advanced practice nurse's application of the Stetler model for research utilisation in improving bereavement care. *Oncology Nursing Forum*; 21: 4, 720–724.

Hicks, C. (1995) The shortfall in published research: a study of nurses' research and publication activities. *Journal of Advanced Nursing*; 21: 594–604.

Hicks, C., Hennessy, D. (1997) Mixed messages in nursing research: their contribution to the persisting hiatus between evidence and practice. *Journal of Advanced Nursing*; 25: 595–601.

Hopps, L.C. (1994) The development of research in nursing in the United Kingdom. *Journal of Clinical Nursing*; 3: 199–204.

Hunt, J. (1981) The process of translating research findings into nursing practice. *Journal of Advanced Nursing*; 6: 189–194.

Hunt, J. (1987) Indicators for nursing practice: the use of research findings. *Journal of Advanced Nursing*; 12: 101–110.

Inman, U. (1975) *Towards a Theory of Nursing Care*. London: Royal College of Nursing.

Kajermo, K.N., Norstrun, G., Krusebrant, A. et al (1998) Barriers to and facilitators of research utilisation, as perceived by a group of registered nurses in Sweden. *Journal of Advanced Nursing*; 27: 798–807.

Kitson A., Ahmed, L.B., Harvey, G. et al (1996) From research to practice: one organisational model for promoting research-based practice. *Journal of Advanced Nursing*; 23: 430–440.

Lacey, E.A. (1994) Research utilisation in nursing practice: a pilot study. *Journal of Advanced Nursing*; 19: 987–995.

Lo-Biondo-Woods, G., Haber, J. (1994) *Nursing Research: Critical Appraisal and Utilisation*. (3rd edn). St Louis: C.V. Mosby.

Lomas, J. (1994) Diffusion, dissemination and implementation: who should do what? *Annals of the New York Academy of Sciences* 1994: 226–237.

McIntosh, J. (1995) Barriers to research implementation. *Nurse Researcher*; 2: 4, 83–91.

MacGuire, J.M. (1990) Putting nursing research findings into practice: research utilisation as an aspect of the management of change. *Journal of Advanced Nursing*; 15: 614–620.

Mead, D. (1996) Using nursing initiatives to encourage the use of research. *Nursing Standard*; 10: 19, 33–36.

Meah, S., Luker, A., Cullum, N.A. (1996) An exploration of midwives' attitudes to research and perceived barriers to research utilisation. *Midwifery*; 12: 2, 73–84.

Morgan, J. (1985) *The Police Experience: Dissemination of Research Findings in Social Work*. Report of a seminar on January 27/28, University of Bristol, England.

Mulhall, A. (1995) Nursing research: what difference does it make? *Journal of Advanced Nursing*; 21: 576–583.

Newham, D.J. (1997) Physiotherapy for best effect. *Physiotherapy;* 83: 1, 5–11.

Nightingale, F. (1980 [1859]) *Notes on Nursing*. London: Churchill Livingstone.

O'Connor, B.B. (1995) *Healing Traditions: Alternative Medicine and the Health Professions*. Philadelphia: University of Philadelphia Press.

Parahoo, K. (1988) Funding nursing research. *Senior Nurse*; 8: 9/10, 12–14.

Pettengill, M.M., Gillies, D.A., Clark, C.C. (1994) Factors encouraging and discouraging the use of nursing research findings. *Image – the Journal of Nursing Scholarship*; 26: 2, 143–147.

Rodgers, S. (1994) An exploratory study of research utilisation by nurses in general medical and surgical wards. *Journal of Advanced Nursing*; 20: 904–911.

Salvage, J. (1998) Evidenced based practise: a mixture of motives. *Nursing Times Research*; 3: 6, 406–418.

Sheehan, J. (1986) Nursing research in Britain: the state of the art. *Nurse Education Today*; 6: 3, 3–10.

Short De-Graff, M. (19??) Times of change in science, health care and research. *Spring;* 17: 2, 75–79.

Short De-Graff, M. (1994) Critical assessment of qualitative research. *Occupational Therapy Journal of Research*; 14: 75–76.

Smith, J.P. (1996) The role of nursing journals in the advancement of professional nursing. *Journal of Advanced Nursing;* 23: 12–16.

Smith, R. (1991) Where is the wisdom? (editorial). *British Medical Journal;* 303: 798–799.

Smith, R. (1993) Filling the lacuna between research and practice: an interview with Michael Peckham. *British Medical Journal;* 307: 1403–1407.

Stephens, L.C., Selig, C.L., Jones, L. et al (1992) Research application: teaching staff nurses to use library search strategies. *The Journal of Continuing Education in Nursing*; 23: 1, 24–28.

Stocking, B. (1992) Promoting change in clinical care. *Quality in Health Care*; 1: 56–60.

Styles, M.M. (1982) *On Nursing Toward a New Endowment*. St Louis: C.V. Mosby.

Thomas, E. (1985) Attitudes towards nursing research among trained nurses. *Nurse Education Today*; 5: 1, 18–21.

Tibbles, L., Sanford, R. (1994) The research journal club: a mechanism for research utilisation. *Clinical Nurse Specialist;* 8: 1, 23–26.

Tierney, A. (1998) The politics of the NHS R&D agenda. *Nursing Times Research*; 3: 6, 419–420.

Titchen, A., Binnie, A. (1993) Research partnerships in collaboration: action research in nursing. *Journal of Advanced Nursing*; 18: 858–865.

Tornquist, E.M., Funk, S.G., Champagne, M.T. (1995) Research utilisation: reconnecting research and practice, AACN. *Clinical Issues*; 6: 1, 105–109.

United Kingdom Central Council for Nurses, Midwives and Health Visitors (1992) *Code of Professional Conduct*. London: UKCC.

Vaughan, B., Edwards, M. (1995) *Interface Between Research and Practice: Some Working Models*. London: King's Fund Centre.

Veeramah, V. (1995) A study to identify the attitudes and needs of qualified staff concerning the use of research findings in clinical practice within mental health care settings. *Journal of Advanced Nursing*; 22: 855–861.

Walshe, K., Ham, C., Appleby, J. (1995) Given in evidence. *Health Service Journal*; 29: June, 28–29.

Watt, G.C.M. (1993) The chief scientist reports: making research make a difference. *Health Bulletin*; 51: 3, 187–195.

Webb, C. (1990) Partners in research. *Nursing Times*; 86: 32, 40–44.

Wright, A., Brown, P., Sloman, R. (1996) Nurses' perceptions of the value of nursing research for practice. *Australian Journal of Advanced Nursing;* 13: 4, 15–18.

Yorkshire Health (1991) *Developing the Research Resource in Nursing and the Therapy Professions*. Harrogate: Yorkshire Regional Health Authority.

Index